THE WASTE
DETECTIVES

METHODS AND TECHNIQUES
for CTOs to Improve Flow, Increase Value and
Boost Profitability in a Large-Scale Transformation

BRIAN HOOKER and **RICHARD MOIR**

To my wife Anne for her love, support and encouragement.

—Richard Moir

ACKNOWLEDGEMENTS

Anne Moir
Gareth Hampson
Graham Southorn
John Seddon
Lizzy Leyshon
Mark Paull

CONTENTS

INTRODUCTION

THE ORGANISATION YOU WORK FOR IS wasting at least 50% of its capacity. It could even be as high as 70%. For a company in the middle of a digital transformation journey, this is bad news. Your organisation needs to be adaptive to deliver meaningful products to customers as quickly as possible to maintain or grow market share. Waste isn't in the plan.

As CTO, you are key to the success of your company's digital transformation project. But how do you get rid of waste? The answer sounds simple: limit the work-in-progress (WIP). But that's hard because waste isn't easy to find. You could say that it's hiding in plain sight, camouflaged by the psychology of both individuals and teams and masked by your existing processes.

You'd be forgiven for thinking that Agile working methods were supposed to be the answer to this. But what you will find is that even after setting up workflows with initiatives, epics and user stories, the flow is repeatedly blocked. Worse still, teams have no idea of the scale of the problem. And once you multiply this across all the teams in the organisation, it can be a whole lot bigger than you thought.

While the scale of waste can drive you to despair, knowing about the problems enables you to act. What if you could identify the most common system conditions (blockers) of waste? Wouldn't it be great for any given team's motivation if their work was not blocked all of the time? From a wider, organisational point of view, you will be able to deliver more products to customers. That means increasing value and releasing at pace, enabling your transformation journey to push onto the next level.

Reading this book will give you a framework to remove waste and increase flow for no additional transformation budget. We will provide you with a step-by-step guide and techniques to implement within your organisation. By the end, you will:

1. Understand the need for waste data in teams.
2. Know the types of resistance you can expect.
3. Know how to establish a workflow.
4. Understand how to flag and capture waste data.
5. Sense the impact of waste on your organisation.
6. Be able to identify the top blockers.
7. Understand the Product Owner's perspective on waste.
8. Know how to influence leadership on the importance of waste.
9. Have problem-solving techniques for removing waste from your organisation.

This book came about as a result of our work with large organisations like yours. What we've found is that many traditional organisations that are in the process of becoming adaptive simply weren't doing it right. They weren't focused on removing blockages and waste, although they were keen to track them as risks and issues.

Over the years, we have discovered that the main problems are moving the blocked work into a blocked status and then effectively ignoring it, often via a general chat update in the daily stand-up. There's often a complete lack of knowledge about the types of waste and blockers and the amount of delivery capacity it saps from teams and tribes. Waste can sap a large percentage of your delivery capacity. That's why, through our consulting, we developed the framework you hold in your hands to find and remove waste in order to increase capacity.

We are a team: Brian Hooker and Richard Moir. Brian has many years' experience in transformation roles, from system engineering and analysis to coaching. He's worked with a range of software companies, including suppliers of single products and providers of bespoke enterprise solutions. Richard was a commissioned officer in the British Army before spending many years in business change. Later, he moved into consultancy and the world of Agile and Systems Thinking.

Together, we are The Waste Detectives and we've joined forces to develop a highly scalable waste removal method. It can be used in Agile, adaptive organisations in the middle of their transformation journey, or for those about to start. We work with people like you—Chief Technical Officers (CTO) who are at the beating heart of transformation programmes.

We have been on this journey together for a while and we are still learning about waste, and finding it interesting too. By writing this book, we hope to pass on our insights and hopefully gain some insights from you—our readers in the Agile profession. We'd love to hear about your experiences so please do contact us via our website, www.thewastedetectives.com.

So join us on our mission to sniff out and remove waste and increase flow. We truly believe our methodology will prove to be a game-changer for you and your organisation.

CHAPTER 1

WHY WORRY ABOUT WASTE?

HAVING ARRIVED IN A NEW ORGANISATION or been promoted to CTO, your first task is to get up to speed on the company's current technology stack, personnel, agility and ability to deliver at pace. All of these go into the creation of a product that's meaningful to the customer and delivered when they want it.

Initially, everything seems fine. Reporting metrics are understood and costs and budgets are known and tracking at an acceptable level. Your organisation has been delivering products to customers for years, there's Agile methodology in place, and teams are using Kanban boards and Jira.[1] The customers are happy, the teams are happy, and the organisation assumes that all is well.

But from your perspective, the flow rate is too slow. Worryingly, it's slow compared to that of your competitors, but the reasons for this aren't obvious. Frustratingly, you cannot put your finger on the root cause of the problem.

Delving a little deeper into these measurements and the risk records, you spot instances of resources not being available, resources being reassigned to more pressing demands, or technology simply not working. All of which causes delays—delays that sap your organisation's capacity to deliver at pace and ultimately make it less competitive than its peers.

This is waste. Having waste in your organisation increases the work-in-progress (WIP) and adds to the amount of capacity that is being sapped from your transformation programme. Indeed, in *The Art of Doing Twice the Work in Half the Time*, Jeff Sutherland estimates that up to 75% of capacity can be lost as a result.

In this book, we will give you a mechanism to identify and remove waste—one that you can embed at scale throughout your organisation. Doing so will decrease frustration and increase productivity. Flow rates will go up, delivering more products at no extra cost and increasing the organisation's capacity for transformation.

But before we can tackle waste, let's look at how it's defined and the different types of waste that you'll encounter.

TYPES OF WASTE IN SOFTWARE DELIVERY

Waste is downtime in production. This downtime is the time in which the product (work) is not progressing towards being consumed, or usable, by the customer. In other words, it is wasted capacity. In software delivery terms, we can define seven types of waste, which are shown in Table 1.1.

A number of professionals in the industry sometimes refer to an additional state of waste known as 'unutilised talent' but we will not cover this eighth type in this book. We'll assume that you're already familiar with Agile terms including user story (the smallest unit of work), epics (sets of stories) and initiatives (multiple epics).

Type of waste	Description
Defect	A bug or other issue in a user story or task that prevents it from being delivered to the customer.

Relearning	Picking up a task or user story that had previously been blocked. This takes a relearning time to understand the task or user story again in order to continue and complete.
Delays	The time a piece of work is on hold, blocked, or waiting to be worked on. It is time lost to work not being progressed, which is the number of days/hours a user story or task is not being worked on and thus not delivering the meaningful product the customer requires. Your resource capacity is not being focused on the value required to release at pace.
Handoffs	The unnecessary movement of work between teams. The work has to be handed off to another team or third party in order to complete it. These are effectively dependencies on other teams within the organisation or external companies. This is a situation where the feature team or tribe does not have the capability within the team to complete all of the work, thus handing off the work to a specialist technical team or, in some cases, to a third party. These hand-offs or dependencies, if not picked up and acted upon by the other party, cause a delay in delivering and completing the work as a whole.
Partially done work	Software that has been written but not deployed. This could also be uncompleted user stories that haven't been completed. This can be caused by overestimating the amount of time it will take, but also where user stories have tasks that have been blocked. This can be shown on a Kanban or Jira board where a user story has tasks left unfinished or an epic where one or more user stories have not been completed. This incomplete, partially completed work can sap capacity and not deliver the value needed by the customer. This delay can be a result of waste blockers in your system of change.

under?

Task switching	Resources are deployed to work on multiple tasks at once, rather than focusing on finishing a task and picking up the next one. Task switching can cause conflicting priorities and impact the end-to-end sequence of work that enables a team to deliver value.
Extra features	This is creating more features than customers require, then delaying the release of a new version until all the extra features are ready to deploy. This can happen when teams start work on an epic or user story and then keep pulling in more work into the epic as stories, or tasks into user stories. By doing this, teams are making the delivery of product to customers slower, making a feedback loop longer to get knowledge from customers.

Table 1.1 The seven types of waste

Having defined waste, let's look at an example of waste in action. Picture a software engineer who needs access to a specialist data resource to complete a user story. However, that resource is not available. What are the consequences for that piece of work and the behaviour it drives?

Once the software development code stops being written, it causes a waste state of "Delay". The data specialist in another team is not available to complete the task on the user story for the software engineer. This causes the user story not to progress, causing waste via the "Handoffs" waste state.

The software engineer has task-switched to another piece of work, causing a waste state of 'Task switching'. The consequence of this is that the work that was most valuable for the customer has stopped, the work-in-progress (WIP) has increased, and the software engineer has picked up a new task.

Research suggests that it takes 15 minutes to get up to speed to perform a task.[2] Putting a task down and restarting it from scratch takes a further 25 minutes. This equates to 40 minutes each time it happens.

This may not seem like much, but if you scale it up across a large organisation, teams could get demotivated. and capacity and budgets are sapped by delays and wasted time.

As a CTO, you may be thinking that all this makes sense but what can I do to help my organisation remove this waste, increase capacity and deliver meaningful products to customers more quickly?

In this book, we will help you do just that. With the help of this book, you can put in a framework to identify and study the seven waste states above. It will give you visibility of three types of waste, an indication of two types, and knowledge of the consequences of the other two.

The types of waste that are visible in an organisation if you know how to measure them are:

- Delays
- Partially done work
- Handoffs

Two other types of waste can be identified from their indirect impact. These are:

- Task switching
- Relearning

In the rest of this book, we will show you how you can identify these five types of waste and address their root cause. In the process, it will improve your organisation's transformational capacity to become more adaptive.

The consequence of the blocked/waste work is potentially connected to the following types of waste:

- Defects
- Extra features

Even if you think your current reporting metrics are satisfactory, your organisation could be losing vital capacity due to waste, which reduces capacity and slows the delivery of products to customers. Competitors with less waste, meanwhile, will have the ability to deliver more products more quickly and at lower cost.

As you can see, there's no time to waste! Let's continue our journey in the next chapter by exploring the impact of data on waste.

TAKEAWAYS

⇨ Even if your current reporting metrics are satisfactory, your organisation could be losing vital capacity due to waste.

⇨ Waste results in products being delivered to customers more slowly.

⇨ Waste results in capacity being reduced.

⇨ Competitors with less waste will be able to deliver more products more quickly at lower cost, giving them a competitive advantage.

CHAPTER 2

TEAMS NEED DATA LIKE FISH NEED WATER

"In God we trust, all others must bring data!"
—W. Edwards Deming

WHEN AN ORGANISATION BEGINS A TRANSFORMATION journey, teams may not understand the data they require to be adapted to the needs and desires of customers. The same is often true of the data required for continuous improvement in an Agile environment. Often, the first step in tackling this issue involves an empirical approach to identify the data needed to evaluate actions and enable learning.[1]

We've experienced this lack of understanding at first hand. In one organisation, we came across a team that had well-established physical boards to visualise their work. The boards had been set up by Ruth, the leader of the feature team and an experienced Scrum Master.[2] Ruth was content with how her team was operating, delivering items of work to the customer every two weeks. But, unknown to her, there was a mass of waste in the team. Ruth's lack of knowledge about which data could help her team, and how to get it, prevented her from getting the team attuned and sensitive to the waste and the conditions that caused it.

When we first met her, Ruth's organisation was two years into a large-scale transformation programme. Her team had moved from a siloed and 'job family' based waterfall approach to delivering changes using the Scrum framework, Kanban boards and Jira. Of course, things didn't always go as planned. And when they hit obstacles and found their work blocked, they moved the ticket into the blocked column. They pivoted away from the blocked work, and switched to the next piece of work.

Previously, the organisation was using waterfall and handed off work between the job families to produce project deliveries for customers, causing hand-off delays and loss of knowledge. These job families could have included:

- Business analysts
- Data analysts
- Business architects
- Solution architects
- Software developers
- Test managers
- Test engineers

Typically, one job family type would have to produce a document, then hand it over to the next job type to perform the next piece of work in a waterfall sequence. They would deliver everything to the customer in one go at the end. In some instances, this was the first time the customer had experienced the product.

Back at the daily stand-up, Ruth fulfilled her role as Scrum Master and coordinated the ceremony using the tried and tested structure:

- What did you do yesterday?
- What are you doing today?
- Any blockers?

The stand-up meetings demonstrated that the team were constantly engaged in purposeful work. They were happy, motivated and empowered, and it showed. However, the blocked work was increasing. Although it was discussed by the team each day, the Scrum Master, the team and the Product Owner seemed oblivious to the consequences of allowing work to stagnate in the blocked state. Collectively, they had no awareness of how long the work had been blocked nor why the team were not able to progress work that was blocked.

The severity of the problem was revealed when the team's Agile coach spotted that some tickets had been blocked for almost 100 days! The team had no idea that some of the work they had started had been stalled for that long, despite a daily ceremony in which blockers were mentioned. By allowing individuals to stop when blocked and pick up something else, the team's policy was essentially to keep individuals busy. This ensured that individuals, and therefore the team, operated in a resource-efficient way. However, the value released to the customer had slowed. By increasing the number of Jira tickets being blocked, the team's work-in-progress (WIP) increased day by day and the flow was inefficient. We'll come back to this issue when we cover workflow in a later chapter.

The team's work was important to the organisation. Their work was ensuring that key regulations were being adhered to, therefore the impact of a delay in meeting these regulations was significant. Delay in delivery was therefore a risk for the organisation. However, this risk was increasing every day. With no progress being made to address what was slowing the team, it was not effectively mitigated and therefore not effectively managed. Without data about the blockers, there was no knowledge of where, how and why work was being held up. The team were oblivious to the trouble they were facing because everyone seemed to be very busy and there was lots of activity!

What we saw in Ruth's team we also observed in many others. When you think about this issue in your own organisation, you can see what's at stake for your transformation programme. None of your teams knows what is stopping them from delivering, and the total amount of work underway is continually growing. There is an ever-increasing amount of things being done but delivery is getting slower. Your delivery risks are not understood and therefore not being mitigated. In short, the situation is out of control.

You are also unaware of problems in the work and engagement with third-party suppliers. The original assumptions and business case for outsourcing the work have been undermined, so the true economic consequences are misunderstood. These are the value for money from your suppliers, the costs of delay in delivery, and the cost of inefficiency in the delivery.

You can get a sense of the impact of the problem by comparing it to modelling by Jeff Sutherland, co-creator of Scrum, in his book *The Art of Doing Twice the Work in Half the Time*. The following is based on his work and theory:

- With zero waste, your organisation is maximising 100% of value by working on 1 thing at a time.
- With waste causing work on 2 pieces of work at the same time, 40% is available to the project and 20% is lost to context-switching.
- With waste causing work on 3 pieces of work at the same time, 20% is available to the project and 40% is lost to context-switching.
- With waste causing work on 4 pieces of work at the same time, 10% is available to the project and 60% is lost to context-switching.
- With waste causing work on 5 pieces of work at the same time, 5% is available to the project and 75% is lost to context-switching.

When we worked with Ruth's organisation, our data showed that 50-70% of work was experiencing blockages, and therefore delays, across the many feature teams we engaged with. In other words, large amounts of the transformation budget provided to the CTO was not going toward delivering value to customers. This organisation's results were very similar to Jeff Sutherland's shown above, proving that there was a lot of waste in this part of the organisation.

WHAT CAUSED THE BLOCKAGE

The problem with the organisation designing a blocked column into the workflow is that it caused feature teams to simply park work in the blocked column that had been started but couldn't, for whatever reason, be progressed by that team. As one piece of work is blocked, another is started. The number of items in the blocked column increases, as does the number of items the team is actively engaged with. As a consequence, the total number of items and therefore the total work-in-progress is increasing. The design of the Jira workflow is influencing the behaviour across your organisation.

This behaviour has become part of the culture of the organisation that you are trying to transform. Many feature teams have already learnt and normalised that it is OK to stop working on the work that is most valuable to the organisation's customers. It's OK to simply abandon the work in a blocked status and just have a chat about it at the daily stand-up.

You may also have teams of bean counters (or all-singing, all-dancing Management Information Systems) measuring how many items are blocked at a point in time. This 'information' is provided to you as part of the reporting routine but it's useless. It provides you with a number at a point in time. It is unrelated to the total amount of work; it does not help you understand the trends of the amount of work increasing over time, nor provide insight into what is causing work to be stopped. Not does it tell you the underlying causes having the most detrimental effect on the organisation's performance and making it inefficient.

The origins of this issue can be traced back to the organisation having set off on its transformation journey without putting some key fundamentals in place. The workflow was introduced without sufficiently testing and evaluating its efficacy for a team or variety of teams and the different types of work they undertake. Right from the outset, the organisation had no concept of searching out and understanding what was slowing them down. At the start of the transformation, there was an assumption that the initial design and structure of the transformed organisation was so good that all the work would always flow unhindered!

The issue is common in organisations embarking on transformation journeys. It stems from taking working practices from small teams and, without any evaluation, scaling the practices across all teams. It is a common mistake, and of course, things are always clearer in hindsight. On the plus side, it can be addressed.

WHAT'S THE ALTERNATIVE?

The first step is to engage your transformation consultants or enablers and explain the problem: that you are aware of the impact a blocked column has in increasing WIP and you are keen to gain knowledge of what is holding back your organisation. The key to gaining this insight is to understand what is causing work to be blocked in teams, and then to understand the most common causes across the organisation.

By removing the blocked column from the workflow, teams will develop a greater understanding of what is blocking their work and the impact that is having. Experiments can be run with the blocked column removed from workflows and replaced with mechanisms to mark and gain information (knowledge) on the waste that impacts flow. This enables teams to engage and develop their own mechanisms to achieve this.

These experiments and methods can then form the building blocks for organisational knowledge about what is blocking the completion of work. This, in turn, informs improvements and strategy for the organisation to not only become more adaptive but also to deliver more to customers for the same investment budget.

EXERCISE: FIND DATA TO IDENTIFY BLOCKERS

The purpose of this exercise is to learn what data is needed to identify blockers. This data can then be used to understand the impact that blockers are having, as well as enabling action to address the causes.

First, identify a number of feature teams to be involved in the exercise. In each team, have the individuals within the teams identify all the work they have started but not yet finished. For this exercise, 'finished' is defined as the point when the work/feature is being used by the organisation's customers. Have the team reflect this visually, using a collaboration app or a physical office wall as shown in Figure 2.1.

The team should then organise the physical or virtual tickets on the boards according to how far they have progressed through the stages of work. Note that 'blocked' is not a stage of work. If a feature was still being developed and it experienced a blocker, such as the dev environment being unavailable, the ticket would be placed with all the other work that was still in development.

Figure 2.1 A physical office Kanban Board

Each feature team should then place a marker, such as a red sticky dot, on tickets that are blocked and leave the work in the stage in which the blockage occurred. Have the teams obtain some basic data relating to that feature/work and add the data on the ticket. The type of data we're interested in is:

- Date the ticket was blocked.
- Who (team or role) is blocking the ticket?
- What is blocking the ticket?
- Impact of the ticket being blocked?

The teams should continue with the exercise for a sample period. Once it has been running for a few weeks or months, ask each team to review its board and tickets and to group them based on the reasons they've been blocked. Groupings may form around other teams that support the feature teams in software delivery. They could include those involved in approval or service introduction or technical issues such as automated scripts failing or test data not being available. For each grouping, have the teams quantify how much work has been held up and how long the work has been delayed. Ask the teams to summarise or even quantify the impact of the delays.

This exercise enables teams to:

- Gather information on what is holding them back.
- Identify the most significant causes of why work is not flowing through the system to the customer.
- Describe the consequences of the blockers that will continue to disrupt the flow of work.

The learning from the exercise needs to be shared with leaders and stakeholders that are accountable for, or dependent on, the work of the teams. If the organisation's performance is to improve, action is required. This action needs to happen with rigour and control. It cannot be a 'side of desk' activity. Interventions must be deliberate and intentional.

A WINDOW INTO YOUR ORGANISATION

Once you have carried out the exercise, the feature teams now know what is holding them back. They may even have connected some of the identified causes with their feelings of frustration and dissatisfaction when trying to complete work. They have sensed and understood problems of which they may not even have been aware. The opportunity to improve has become tangible and visible. Members of the feature teams come to work with the aim of doing a good job and can now see how the organisation is holding them back. Now that the issues have been identified, they will expect action to be taken to fix them.

Despite these potential risks and raised expectations, there are positive outcomes from the exercise:

1. Teams have discovered the issues for themselves and are now aware of what is holding them back.
2. Curiosity has been nurtured within teams about the data and improvements.
3. Discussions have started about the blockers, the consequential waste and the resulting impact.
4. Discussions have started between teams and leaders about problems and improvement.

By collecting data on delays, blockages and issues, you establish a window into just how poorly your organisation is functioning. The scale and variety of the problems could be vast and you should prepare yourself for this. On the plus side, you now know what data is important in tackling the issue of blockers.

In this chapter, we've seen that your organisation may have been set up poorly at the outset of the transformation programme. Work-in-progress (WIP) was allowed to increase unchecked, the time to complete work was increasing, and the rate at which value was released to customers was reduced. With blockers and delays remaining unchecked, budget would have been wasted on partly completed and neglected work.

Knowledge of how your organisation works, and what isn't working as intended, provides the power to act on the issues. Applying this knowledge effectively will shift your organisation's performance and its ability to be adaptive, making it capable of delivering meaningful and timely products and services to customers. Not only that, but it will also be a far less frustrating place for colleagues to work.

There is a risk, however. A common reaction is to identify someone to blame and hold accountable but conflict and defensiveness will not enable effective action. In the next chapter, we'll look at ways to manage this and strive for collaboration in problem-solving and improvements.

TAKEAWAYS

⇨ Create curiosity among teams about the need for waste data.

⇨ Allow teams to find waste problems on their own.

⇨ Establish a consistent way of doing it from the ground up.

⇨ Collaboration is key to gaining knowledge.

⇨ Bring the waste data knowledge into the cadences and tie the story into the flow of meaningful products to the customer.

⇨ Focus on the problem you are trying to solve and the benefits it provides to all in the organisation.

CHAPTER 3

RESISTANCE

THERE'S NO GETTING AWAY FROM THE fact that sometimes you'll encounter resistance. In Chapter 2, we met Ruth, the Scrum Master who had previously helped her team set up boards to make their work visible. The problem with the board was that Ruth had included a blocked column in the workflow design. Any work items blocked on their journey through the workflow could be moved into the blocked column.

In this chapter, we'll look at what can happen when you come across similar situations in your own organisation. We'll show you how to approach resistance when you encounter it, the tactics you can employ to win teams round, and how we put these ideas into practice.

The way that Ruth and her team had set up their board seemed perfectly logical to them. Everyone could see how much work was blocked and which work items could not progress. But while we could immediately see the problem, we mishandled the messaging. One of us immediately launched into telling the team the solution they needed to adopt, giving them clear direction to remove the blocked column.

The reaction wasn't what we'd hoped for, to say the least. Ruth's instant response was: "I have been a Scrum Master for two years and have always had a blocked column. It is helpful, and I want to keep it". The room fell silent for a moment or two; a rather awkward silence. We hadn't expected this reaction and the implications were daunting. Was Ruth's response indicative of how our ideas would be received in an organisation of thousands of change professionals and a very large annual change budget? If so, the transformation progress was going to be far slower than we'd imagined.

Before we can get over this hurdle, it's useful to consider how Ruth's organisation had gotten to this point in its large-scale transformation. In the early stages, it had many transformation coaches and hundreds of change agents and thousands of physical boards and electronic Jira boards to manage workflows. All of them were established and running with blocked columns in place. But this also meant that there were thousands of colleagues with no mechanism to accurately measure the flow of their work as it progressed through the workflow states. Nor did they have any mechanism to identify and accurately measure the waste that was impacting and disrupting the flow of their work.

To achieve agility and flow, and optimise the delivery of value at scale, it is highly likely that you'll need the help and support of the organisation's communities of Scrum Masters, Agile or transformation coaches and change agents. Given the importance of flow, we were surprised to learn that almost half the coaches involved in the transformation were reluctant to remove the blocked column. The consequence of this was that the organisation risked having an awful 'halfway house' scenario of multiple team boards with a blocked column and an equal number without one.

A lack of coherence and consistency across an organisation in dealing with blockages not only limits improvement for teams, but also complicates the alignment of work between teams. This can also impact the efforts of the teams to identify limiting constraints or system conditions.[1] Typically, you can expect to hit widespread resistance when attempting to deploy even a basic concept across a large enterprise transformation journey.

So why are blocked columns used and why is it such a problem?

HOW AND WHY BLOCKED COLUMNS ARE USED

Many Scrum Masters are taught the basic concepts of their craft within the context of a single team, including the use of Kanban, with boards structured to include a blocked column. This learning context and structure creates a norm for learners right from the outset. It's the equivalent of learning to drive with the learner continually leaving a hand on the gear stick. Unhelpful habits are formed and the longer the habit persists, the harder it is to break.

Learners may be getting to grips with Kanban but they are not truly learning about flow and therefore the importance of limiting WIP. Consequently, they are not learning how to apply practices that optimise flow and particularly how this is done at scale across a large organisation. Being able to optimise flow is essential for multi-million-pound businesses if they are to scale their agile efforts and become more adaptable.

With blocked columns established as the norm, teams develop the habit of moving a physical or electronic ticket into blocked status. They grow comfortable talking about the blocked work as a collective group, or status. This behaviour becomes the status quo. So why is the blocked column so appealing and what logic maintained its use? Why, for example, was the use of the blocked column never challenged in a retrospective or subject to improvement efforts?[1]

From our observations, we found that:

- The blocked column was essentially used as a 'car park', i.e. something to come back to later, which eased the issue of having insufficient time to problem-solve.

- This gave the teams a sense of control as they could quickly and easily account for work that was not going to be completed, and therefore focus on the velocity and burndown of the remaining work.
- For individuals and teams, there were no consequences from a build-up of items in the blocked column, nor to an absence of problem-solving.
- When work was put into a blocked column, it was easier for the team to pick up another piece of work than fix the cause of the work being stopped. This then became one of the causes of work-in-progress (WIP) increasing, flow debt increasing and lead or cycle time increasing, therefore contributing to problems in the flow of the work.[2]
- The focus of management that was responsible for the teams was primarily on activity and delivery rather than improvement.[3]
- With the prevailing focus on activity and delivery, teams and individuals didn't feel safe to stop and fix problems.
- Organisations track risks, rather than focusing on dealing with the problems.

Part of the reason for this boils down to culture: the norms that are the accepted and common patterns of behaviour. They are shaped by a logic that manifests itself through policies, processes, structures and roles. John Seddon, the inventor of the Vanguard Method, describes these as system conditions. In the organisations we observed, we found that:

- Problem-solving was not designed into roles, processes, routines or planning. As such, it was not given importance and became a lower priority.
- Preoccupation with delivery, costs, and satisfying internal stakeholders manifested as a fear of holding up work that was on the backlog and had been prioritised.

- Product owners that had come through a project management track often maintained their learnt focus on the completion of activity needed for the completion of the change; working on problems was rarely elevated above working through backlog items.

Just as the norm of employing a blocked column is established for an individual team, it is also recursive and is established as a norm across the organisation. Blocked columns become common features on the boards of all teams. This is reinforced when organisations standardise or align their workflows to the states that are commonly used by teams. As a consequence, business management or management information (MI) teams generate metrics and reports on the quantity of work being blocked at a particular point in time. This then creates a norm for leaders and senior management so that volumes of blocked work are abstracted from the flow or the work.

Blocked work, therefore, becomes an isolated metric. Forgive the grisly analogy, but only measuring the quantity of blocked work is akin to knowing how much blood a patient has lost but not knowing why they are bleeding. Knowing the number of work items in the blocked column does not help the leaders understand where, in the organisational flow, the systemic and predictable problems exist that are affecting current work. Without visibility, leaders will be unable to take any corrective action and today's problems will therefore be tomorrow's problems too.

Transformation coaches and Agile coaches can be made up of individuals from a wide variety of backgrounds with skills and capabilities in a variety of areas. Just because you have a transformation coach and an Agile coach doesn't mean they have the right skills. Many have built their knowledge and expertise as Scrum Masters, but not all have a thorough understanding of the concept of flow, nor been fortunate enough to explore the concept through GetKanBan.[4]

Since coaches help teams set up whiteboards and Jira projects, teams and individuals then become committed to the norm of using 'blocked' columns. With these established in the workflows and in use by the teams, greater numbers of colleagues settle into the norm and habitual use of the blocked work state. By challenging the norm of 'blocked' as a legitimate work state, this can appear to challenge the coaches' guidance and even their expertise, resulting in them feeling that their reputation and expert power is at risk.[5] However, with some care, this can be positioned as another learning opportunity for individuals. For organisations to be adaptive, individuals need to continually be in a learning mode, being self-aware of the feelings we go through to accept and embed change, as shown in Figure 3.1.

Figure 3.1 Change curve feelings

WHO BENEFITS FROM THE BLOCKED COLUMN?

It is certainly true that teams using the blocked column can instantly visualise the work that cannot progress, but that is as far as the benefit goes. The benefit, therefore, is limited to acting only on individual pieces of work. There is little opportunity to take action to prevent the recurrence of the blockage on future pieces of work.

Let's follow this through with a scenario. A piece of work enters the 'in-progress' state but it then becomes blocked. In practice, this means that the work item cannot progress further without some additional action. Typically, teams deem work as being blocked when the necessary action is beyond the scope of the team to achieve, e.g. they need some sort of sign off or they need to access a particular environment but have to wait their turn to get access. Until the necessary action is taken, the work item will therefore remain in the same incomplete state, and if no action is taken, it will remain in perpetuity.

From the Lean Software Development perspective, the point the delay occurs is when waste has occurred.[6] The obvious type of waste is 'waiting'. However, there are second-order types of waste that consequently occur, such as 'partially done work' and 'task switching', while the waiting itself may actually be caused by 'extra features'.[7] The flow of the team's work is disrupted from the point that the blockage and waste occur. Following the established norm, the ticket representing the work item is therefore moved from the 'in-progress' state to the 'blocked' state. A common response to this is that the team brings in a new piece of work so that there is always sufficient work available.

Although the team is able to visualise the work in the blocked state, the work can become forgotten. Maybe it is overlooked as everyone knows it is blocked. Until it is unblocked, it does not warrant attention. It may be that the phenomenon of attentive blindness is at play.[8] While the team is keenly focused on the work that is being actively progressed and in a dynamic state, the blocked work becomes the gorilla amidst a basketball team. Typically, there is no mark or record of when the work became blocked, nor the reason as to why it was blocked, let alone the root cause of the blockage.

Every time a team introduces a new piece of work to 'in progress' in order to backfill one that has been blocked, they are actually increasing the total work-in-progress (WIP) by one. Increasing the WIP in a system has the effect of slowing down the release of meaningful products to customers. This is something we will explore further in a forthcoming chapter.

Over time, the blocked column becomes a dumping ground for items of work that are too difficult to progress or that have hit dependency or system conditions outside of the team's control.[9] This, in turn, slows the release of value, delaying the delivery of products. In its quest to optimise flow and improve cycle time, the organisation is unable to obtain accurate and predictable data. With work being moved from a status such as 'in-progress' to 'blocked', the record of reality is lost. The organisation loses the ability to understand the true duration of time for which the work has been 'in-progress'. From the perspective of the 'in-progress' state, the stopwatch has been stopped but for the customer awaiting delivery of the product, the clock continues to run...

We've now seen why the blocked column is commonly used and explored the disadvantages and negative consequences. Let's now look at the alternative.

ALTERNATIVE TO BLOCKED COLUMN AND BENEFITS

The alternative to a blocked column is to simply keep the work in its true state in the workflow. Even when the work is blocked, it remains in the workflow state in which the blockage occurred. The benefits of this are:

- The work constantly remains visible to the team.
- The cycle time for work items reflects the actual elapsed time that work has been in the work state.
- The work item remains a visible part of the WIP count and prevents the team from pulling in more work just because the work item has been blocked.

By taking this approach, the Scrum Master, Product Owner and Agile Coach are forced to confront the question of why the work is blocked, igniting conversations about how to resolve the blockage and what has caused it. The continued study of what gets blocked and what causes the blockages accumulates knowledge about how the team is performing as a system of change and helps crystallise an understanding about the waste that is degrading the system's performance.

As soon as a ticket is blocked, a learning opportunity opens. The work item must be left in the work state in which the blockage occurs, and from there the learning for the team and the Scrum Master can then start. Key data can now be gathered, such as:

- Date the work item became blocked.
- What or who has blocked the progress of the work item.
- Why the work item is blocked.
- Impact and consequence of the work item being blocked in terms of value release to customers and the organisation.

This approach, and the opportunity to gather information, has benefits for both the team and organisation. By gathering data over time for all blocked work items, the data can be grouped and patterns identified relating to the common circumstances and causes of why work items are getting blocked. This quickly begins to turn data into actionable information, which is immediately available to the Scrum Master, Product Owner and development team.[10]

IMPLEMENTING AN ALTERNATIVE

Learning how to address blockages and get quicker at spotting and removing them successfully will, of course, remove waste. But while this sounds great, it only provides a limited amount of benefit because the problem recurs and you end up having to solve it over and over again.

Imagine driving your car to work. Every morning, you go out to your car and discover a flat tyre that prevents you from starting your journey. You could, of course, simply inflate the tyre and get to work. But by accepting the fact that you must solve the same problem each morning, you have essentially introduced a policy that it is OK to solve it repeatedly. The alternative is to understand the root cause of why your car has a flat tyre each morning.

Chris Argyris, a business theorist from Harvard Business School, described this approach as the difference between single-loop and double-loop learning.[11] Single-loop questions help you get better at dealing with the presenting problem, whereas double-loop questions confront the policies that sustain the problem. In our simple car example, double-loop questions are: 'Why does my car have a flat tyre each morning?' and 'What is repeatedly affecting my tyre?'. Successfully answering these questions creates a different set of actions from answering single-loop questions.

A more corporate example can be found in customer-facing call centres, where the volume of calls repeatedly exceeds the capacity (i.e. the number of operatives handling the calls). This scenario results in longer queues of customers waiting to speak to an operative, and therefore longer wait times for customers. This often leads to an increase in calls where the customer is no longer willing to wait and so ends the call. Such 'abandoned calls' have an impact on customer satisfaction. Typical single-loop questions and actions applied in this scenario are:

- How can we reduce the time it takes to service the customer and therefore the call duration?
- How can we reduce the number of calls by encouraging customers to use alternative channels?
- How can we reduce the manual effort of the operatives in the call by using automation?

Double-loop questions in this scenario are:

- Is the daily volume of calls higher than expected and is human resource capacity used to deal with calls calculated?
- Has the daily volume of calls risen over time?
- Do all the customers that call want to make their call?
- Why are customers calling us?

The last questions are often the most insightful. The intuitive response is often, "Of course, they want access to our product/service".

However, there are often a surprising number of customers that are calling because something didn't happen or didn't occur in the manner that matters to the customer. This is a phenomenon that John Seddon describes as 'failure demand'.[12]

For our purposes in looking at blockages, if a cause has been identified then any subsequent occurrence of that cause should be considered a failure demand. Its occurrence is unwanted and generates effort and use of capacity that could be prevented. Once failure demand has been identified, it provides an opportunity for improvement. That starts by asking the double-loop questions and identifying actions that remove the root causes of delays.

Stopping failure demand from recurring also removes the frustrations experienced by team members when their work is blocked. Consequently, removing the failure demand also improves team morale. Releasing the capacity that would otherwise be spent dealing with the blockages helps your organisation become more adaptive and increases the flow of meaningful products to the customer.

Earlier in the chapter, we set out the two problems of moving away from using the blocked column and the resistance you will experience when trying to help teams, change agents and leaders to abandon it. Now you know what to do about the first problem, let's look at the second one: tackling resistance.

HOW TO APPROACH RESISTANCE

There are many change models that may help when proposing changes to existing practices and approaches.[13] We have learned that change happens by working with teams in a way that allows them to learn through their own experiences. You are very unlikely to convince people to change their minds. You can, however, create circumstances and learning opportunities that enable them to convince themselves to change their minds.[14] Merely talking about workflow states, flow and waste won't cut it. Experience, valid data and informed choice are much better enablers for individuals to undergo a change in thought and action.[15]

Valid data does not always need to be directly drawn from the work that individuals and teams are engaged in—that is where the proof of the pudding lies! Instead, simulations or 'gamification' can be effective at helping people get new data through their own experiences. GetKanBan.com is a great example of this and has some fantastic materials that enable people to build their understanding of flow and WIP. Teams can visualise and safely experiment with workflow structures, designs and policies. This, of course, includes simulating approaches with no blocked column to experience the impact and benefit of working without it in the safe confines of the game. All of the teams with which we used this technique have benefited greatly from the experience and significantly built their knowledge about flow.

Using the structure and rapid feedback loops incorporated in the game provides an opportunity to build on the experience of limiting WIP and removing blocked columns. As work starts to get blocked in the game, the opportunity arises to pique the curiosity of Product Owners and teams, enhancing their desire to understand and remove the impediments.

These immersive and experiential approaches rapidly enable the team, Scrum Master and Product Owner to see how much waste is in their system of change. This can be a real shock to them. After all, the teams and leaders will probably have invested time and emotional energy in their current workflow and policies and nobody wants to hear how ugly their baby is. Psychologists describe this as a cognitive dissonance.[16] As human beings, we are not designed to maintain two competing and contradictory beliefs. When cognitive dissonance is experienced, we can either rationalise away the data that triggered the cognitive dissonance or accept it and take action that is coherent with the new data and perspective.

Some of the change models, such as the Kubler-Ross Change Curve, reflect the impact that new data and its impact can have on individuals.[17]

Normative experiences are a key part of the learning process and cognitive dissonance cannot be designed out. Instead, it can be anticipated and supported by leaders and coaches. The greatest enabler is that once teams have the facts, they can act using that data, which in turn provides them with knowledge.

At this point, you have teams, Scrum Masters and Product Owners with you. However, the focus then switches to the fundamental problems that need to be addressed. As a collective, you can now see the dependencies. Teams holding up the flow of work, internal processes not working as expected, and external suppliers not working effectively with you are some of the most common. For teams investing time and effort in recording key data relating to blockers and waste, this is a key point where momentum is vital. Capturing data relating to the waste is necessary but insufficient. Frustration for the team will remain as long as there are causes of waste.

TACTICS TO HELP OVERCOME RESISTANCE

Resistance to change can undoubtedly be a tough challenge to crack. Having explored why resistance occurs and some of the theory that helps you deal with it, here are some of the tactics we have learnt through experience:

- Present to as many teams as possible.
- Identify coaches who are curious.
- Be open about the purpose.
- Be available to anyone who is curious.
- Bring in anyone who shows they are keen to help and has the capability, and make them part of the journey.
- Reach out to Scrum Master communities.
- Tell the story of what you are trying to achieve through podcasts and vlogs.

These are all tactics that may prove helpful; the key effect we are seeking is to enable people to have a being in the work, known as a normative learning experience.[18] Remember, you cannot convince people to change their minds, you can only create conditions that will help people to convince themselves to change their minds.

At the beginning of this chapter, we recalled our experience with Ruth the Scrum Master and her team. Having experienced the immediate pushback from Ruth to our advice, we quickly moved to an alternative option. We proposed a demonstration of our suggested course of action, backed up with an offer of free coffee and cake (our usual tactic to attract an audience!). Allowing the team to observe for themselves the concept we were proposing did generate, as you would expect, lots of questions: "Why do it?", "What is in it for us?" and "Who is going to do what with the data?"

These are typical of the challenges that are voiced when groups are confronted with a proposed change. This group reflection and open discussion is an important part of the process and allows everyone to air their views and get to a collective, agreed-upon view on the purpose of the action and what it is you are trying to achieve. On our transformation journey, it took several months to get just one of the many Product Owners in our part of the organisation to remove the blocked column.

Where you meet complete resistance, don't let it stop you and don't get dragged into a protracted exchange of views. Go around the point of resistance and continue the journey. At times, you may interact with people who do not like it and openly express the fact, but this could be due to any number of reasons beyond your influence and control. Sometimes you need to don your armour and carry on, keeping in mind your overarching goal to improve the flow of value in the organisation.

As your teams and the organisation become interested in moving away from blocked columns, it is time to tackle the next big challenge that emerges—dealing with how to flag waste, as we'll see in the next chapter.

TAKEAWAYS

⇨ The blocked column is your nemesis.

⇨ Bring the conversation back to the question, "What is the problem we are trying to solve?"

⇨ No resistance is personal so return the conversation back to the work.

⇨ Listen to what is being said, as if you will act on it once. You will have to do it many times, or find a way to land the problem statement better.

⇨ Finding open-minded Scrum Masters and Product Owners is key.

⇨ Call out why the organisation and Scrum Masters have been using the blocked column, explaining the problems this causes.

CHAPTER 4

WORKFLOW

CHIEF TECHNOLOGY OFFICERS (CTOS) AND CHIEF Digital Officers embarking on digital transformation programmes face a challenge. Their organisations will have developed policies, processes and mechanisms over many years. Resourcing, deployment and reporting have all been geared to provide visibility and control of progress against targets, budgets and risk.

Implementing a new Agile method will often cause conflict with existing structures, policies and processes, and often this happens in ways that are not obvious, visible or expected. You need to recognise that this conflict will occur and that friction will be a fact of life. It cannot be prevented ahead of time. In this chapter, we'll look at how to identify friction and the counter-measures that can minimise it.

The challenge is not merely moving from project delivery to product delivery. It is not as simple as selecting an Agile method and abandoning all previous project management methods, and there are two main reasons for this:

1. Not all changes suit the iterative and emergent approaches that the Agile Manifesto was

designed to address. The changes will address problems (or sat-isfy opportunities) and therefore the nature or type of problem will dictate the most appropriate method and approach for solving it. This concept has been described as 'bounded appli-cability' and is very clearly explained through Dave Snowden's Cynefin framework (Figure 4.4).[1] The organisation may still encounter problems that require a more traditional change delivery response. Organisations therefore face a new chal-lenge; of developing the capability to recognise the nature of the problems they need to address and identifying the most appropriate method to respond.

2. An organisation's project-management method is only one component in the change delivery system. Simply swapping out the current method and replacing it with a new Agile method may be necessary, but it is unlikely to be sufficient to achieve the success and performance expected from a digital transfor-mation. Policies, processes, and mechanisms that were estab-lished to enable traditional project management are likely to conflict with new Agile methods. Growing recognition of this issue has led to the development of Business Agility.[2] Adopting Agile principles impacts more than just the feature and delivery teams, it requires change from many other parts of the organi-sation, including resourcing, HR, investment, finance, and risk. However, simply recognising this fact does not reduce the chal-lenge of such a wholesale change. In reality, it often cannot be achieved in one huge, 'big bang' pivot.

The solution is often perceived as training and up-skilling team members in the new methods—feature teams adopting an Agile method and infrastructure teams adopting DevOps. But even if there is a recognition that adopting these methods will impact other parts of the organisation, it's very unlikely that the changes required could be clearly described in detail. The prospect of making widespread change in the face of potential uncertainties holds huge risk, and this is the reason why the 'big bang' pivot is so unworkable and so unlikely (see Figure 4.1).

Figure 4.1 Potential uncertainties

Now that we've identified that 'big bang' probably isn't going to work, let's move on to look at the scenario at the coal face, with teams eager to get going and be empowered. As CTO, you will understandably not have control over all elements of your organisation. Policies, processes and structures that cause friction in the transformation are probably not under your control. There will also be pressure from executives and the board to get started, show progress and complete the transformation. And yet until teams start to deliver using new methods, you probably won't be able to predict or quantify delays, blockages and waste.

Having some teams start with their new Agile method provides the opportunity to sense and learn about other areas in the organisation that must be involved in the transformation. This can be a key learning phase. However, the prevailing view is likely to be that teams should start using the new Agile method as soon as possible, and so the old adage of "haste makes waste" is proven true.

The first teams in the organisation to make a start will understandably be very eager. They'll sense the empowerment they have been craving for years and the opportunity for the organisation to catch up with others in the start-up world. The potential to deliver ever more meaningful products that customers desire will be tangible. The starting point for these teams is often to attend Agile courses and participate in training. It's at this early point that problems can be created, with empowered teams typically creating workflows based on generic training they've received on basic Agile courses (as shown in Figure 4.2).

Figure 4.2 Basic Kanban board

Each team leverages their new-found freedom and starts to deliver in the way that makes sense to them and best suits the circumstances they work in. Within the team, they will be completing work more quickly, and possibly more of it, than under their previous ways of working. The team's understanding of how to operate in a new paradigm, in a way that they choose, creates a collective muscle memory and requires less conscious effort to maintain new behaviours and habits. This is great for a small organisation with a handful of teams, particularly for those that can release on demand, as envisaged by the effective deployment of Scrum (Figure 4.3). However, your organisation could have thousands of transformational resources and millions of customers. At the early stage of this problem, you would be layering a small Agile component into a large organisation ecosystem.

The teams will generally operate at a story or task level to deliver, while your organisation needs to deliver on purpose and outcomes that typically require a layered structure of initiative—epic—story—task. This connects the organisation's key strategic themes, with customer/user needs and the detailed activity needed to move the organisation toward its goals.

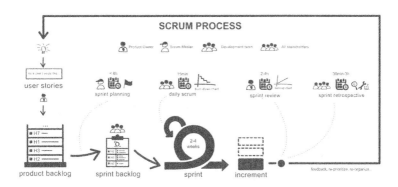

Figure 4.3: Scrum process

Almost immediately, you will encounter a problem. Different teams will define stories to different sizes, so that the effort and duration required to complete a story in one team will be a different order of magnitude in others. In addition, teams will create and adapt their own workflows, so there will be a number of different workflows operating at the story level. After a short time, you will begin to encounter the next level of challenges:

- Teams getting used to parking work that's blocked and increasing their work-in-progress (WIP).
- An inability to measure and improve flow and learn from experience to become more adaptive.
- Different teams can have different workflows, and being empowered is great. However, this causes the teams to have a personal interest in their own implemented workflow.
- The organisation may have no method or policy as to why, what and how measurement should be conducted.
- Any flow metrics that exist are in teams only, making it challenging for the CEO and their leadership teams to connect with, and understand, flow through their organisation.

We've now identified that 'empowerment' builds momentum and energy throughout the organisation. Let's now move on to look at things from an executive perspective.

Executives will expect additional perspectives, and will no doubt expect you to be able to answer questions relating to their interests and preoccupations. Questions around timely delivery of meaningful products to customers might be:

- How does handing work between teams impact our effectiveness in producing products, and is it happening in an efficient manner?
- Where are the biggest problems the organisation needs to solve in order to improve timeliness, effectiveness and efficiency in delivering products?
- What are the critical capabilities, skills and knowledge needed?

- How effective and efficient are our third-party suppliers and partners?
- What information could relationship managers and contract negotiators use for more effective supplier choice and management?

These would be great things to understand before transformations are implemented in the organisation. However, more often than not, the horse has already bolted when these questions start to arise. The reality is that it may not be possible to answer some of them until the transformational journey begins. All the more important, then, that you detect the early symptoms and rapidly learn the answers to these questions.

Although no two organisations are the same, they often have common characteristics and structures. A top-level view of a typical organisation often looks like this:

1. Human Resources.
2. Sales.
3. Risk.
4. Finance.
5. Delivery.
6. Technical Support *(Within the organisation)*.
7. Customer Service.

As CTO, you're likely to have focused on delivery, with the goal of delivering more and quicker to keep pace or get ahead of your competitive market. This functional, reductionist approach to management responsibilities is typical of organisations that remain influenced by the traditional industrial manufacturing management logic as applied by Frederick Winslow Taylor as well as Alfred Sloan.[3] This logic encourages segmentation of duties, accountability and, invariably, focus. Therefore as CTO, you may not have taken other organisational perspectives with you, or even factored them into the strategic transformation goals.

As the transformation grows and develops momentum, questions that may start to arise are shown in Table 4.1:

Organisation area	Types of questions
Human Resources	What is the organisation structure/ design we are heading towards? What resourcing/recruitment is required for the next 12-24 months to move to the new structure/design?
Sales	When am I going to get product 'X' so I can market the theme 'Y'? We have a marketing/advertising campaign lined up for date 'aa/yy/zz'. Will the product be ready in time?
Risk	What governance controls do you have in place? Prove to us you are delivering the new products and changes safely. Can you demonstrate you're operating within the regulator's policies?
Finance	What is your forecast of costs for the next year? Are you meeting the spending targets set out in the organisation's four-year operating plan? What is the business case for the new products you propose and what investment is required? Will we capitalise the new products in the same way that we capitalise projects? Tell us what spend will go on improvements and what spend will be required for operating/maintaining/running the existing infrastructure/platforms/components?
Delivery	When is the feature/initiative going to be delivered? I am unable to see progress as the various teams involved all have different workflows in place! I am under pressure to show why we have spent £10 million. Show me when we are going to release the new product.

Data	What is the scalable data profile? All the teams are doing their own thing; is this uncontrolled? Are we creating data problems? Have we created a new risk?
Customer Service	When is the new product going to be released? What do we need to know to provide support and help to our customers?

Table 4.1 Types of questions to expect from different areas of the organisation

Now that we've identified the types of information and questions that may be asked across the top-level view of the organisation, let's move on and look at an exercise that helps test the workflows via collaboration. Checking a workflow against the questions above is a useful exercise for CTOs.

EXERCISE: MECHANISM TO TEST A WORKFLOW VERSUS QUESTIONS IT NEEDS TO ANSWER

Collaborate and create some workflows on a board with different workflow statuses. Come up with some made-up tasks as a group, adding start and end dates.

Run a few scenarios of work through the board and think of the measurements you could capture. Think back to the organisational area questions earlier in this chapter. How are you going to answer those questions from the workflow you are looking to deploy?

From the point of view of Delivery, they'd want to know when the feature/initiative will be delivered. Plus, they'd be concerned about being unable to see progress because of the different workflows adopted by different teams!

From the perspective of Risk, they want to know the organisation's five worst-performing third-party suppliers. They want to know the cost of delay from those suppliers and they need it now as they are nego-tiating a new contract next week!

Ask yourself if you can answer questions from the different organi-sation areas in Table 4.1. If not, is your workflow suitable!

DOING THINGS DIFFERENTLY

Performing the exercise in this chapter helps you to sense-check your workflow against questions you'd like to answer in the longer term. Let's now look at how doing things differently in a complex domain can cre-ate uncertainty.

Doing things differently invariably generates worry and concern in people impacted by changing the way things are done. The table above demonstrates the sort of inter-connections we must consider when we try to make changes. There are multiple views and needs, and human beings seek information to reduce their fear. That said, operating in, and changing, a complex adaptive system invariably creates uncertainty.

The level of complexity and the competing needs (even conflict!) within the organisation can feel overwhelming. What is required is a foundation or grounding that everyone can relate to; a focus for align-ment that allows evaluation of changes and improvements. Essentially, the transformation is operating in the complex domain and therefore must be a continuous stream of experiments rather than a preordained static plan (see Figure 4.4).[4]

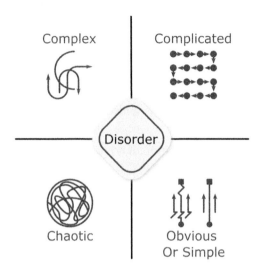

Figure 4.4 Cynefin Framework

Which foundation provides a common interest that's relevant throughout the organisation? The answer actually lies outside it. The organisation may have lots of external stakeholders but it only exists as long as there are customers or users that get value from the products and services it provides. This is as true for not-for-profits as it is for commercial institutions. An organisational preoccupation with value creation for customers, and therefore with the flow of value, provides that common dimension. Using this enables the changes to be evaluated and the organisation reconfigured.

Engaging other organisational areas in the challenge of optimising the flow of value helps re-frame the typical questions shown in Table 4.1. So let's take a closer look at flow and, in particular, the seven types of waste you'll encounter in software development.

FLOW

When we explored how workflows through a team, we saw examples of boards (physical and electronic) that made visible the progress of items being worked on. The columns represent the stages or steps that items progress through until they are completed by the team or, as they are often described, 'Done'!

However, this raises a question. If it is done from the team's perspective, is it done from the customer's perspective? If it is, then the team's visualisation of workflow does indeed represent the flow of value to the customer or user. But often it does not, particularly in large organisations. Other teams will have to complete activity before and after the feature teams have completed their work. If we think of the chain of teams that are required to create and deliver value to customers as a system, at a fundamental level the purpose of that system is simply:

"To deliver a meaningful product to the customer as quickly as possible."

Across the multiple teams involved in achieving this purpose will be activities that are essential for the purpose to be satisfied. However, these activities may be fragmented across different teams. There will also be other activities that are not essential, distracting from the essential activity, using precious capacity and preventing value-creation activity. Both types are likely to have periods of inactivity between them, when no activity is happening on the work item.

The concept of the essential value-creating activity and 'everything else' has its origins in manufacturing and the lean movement. The 'everything else', including the inactivity and delays, was labelled 'waste'. This concept was adapted by the Lean Software Development movement, with Mary and Tom Poppendieck providing an excellent comparison and defining seven types of waste in software development (see Figure 4.5).

Figure 4.5 Waste types in software

As you can see, there are many different types of waste, but they are all detrimental to meeting purpose and can have a significant cumulative effect on how much, and how quickly, work can be completed. As previously highlighted in Chapter 2, waste affects the predictability of when work will be done. It slows the feedback loops that validate that the thing being created does indeed have the effect and create the value that's expected. This is why it is so important that teams are identifying waste when it occurs and that action is taken to address and remove the causes.

Importantly, predicting where waste occurs should be done across multiple teams. A very useful way of doing this is to undertake a collaborative visualisation activity such as Value Stream Mapping.[5] This allows teams, as a collective, to define what the essential value-adding activity is, as well as where the waste is. It helps to identify the impact of the waste and gives the different teams and roles insight into other teams and roles, the difficulties they face, and what they need from other teams to complete their contribution. As CTO, rolling this information upwards, you can get good predictions of where the waste is across multiple teams.

With the collective, end-to-end activity understood, an individual team can then reflect on the workflow they are using to visualise and manage work. It is very unlikely that all the teams will have identical workflows, nor that they will be able to adopt identical workflows. Nor is it likely that a single workflow can be applied to encompass all the activity end-to-end, as many teams will be involved with teams in other end-to-end systems. Two factors that are important for the workflows in each team are:

1. Teams are able to visualise the work that is in progress, which state/stage it is in, whether it is actively being worked on or whether it is waiting to be pulled into the next activity and state in the workflow.
2. Teams have agreed and explicit policies; this enables other teams to understand how that team operates. A team can include reflections on how well they are working to the policies when undertaking retrospectives.

It's not a good idea to rush the task of getting a workflow up and running for Agile feature teams. Instead, think of the peers you will need to engage and provide the information needed to the main components of the organisation. Removing fear from all organisational perspectives, and bringing the whole organisation with you from the start, will soften the pain later on. In the next chapter, we'll get back to practical considerations by examining how to flag waste data.

TAKEAWAYS

⇨ Take a number of stakeholders along with you on the journey.

⇨ Waste data needs to be relevant to the stakeholder to be able to have a conversation about the waste.

⇨ Having inconsistent workflows could prevent you from building a holistic view of your waste data, making it harder to fix problems.

⇨ Teams, tribes and labs need to give you, the CTO, the knowledge to continuously improve the system of change by removing waste from it.

⇨ Be open to hearing about the problems teams, tribes and labs are facing.

CHAPTER 5

FLAGGING WASTE DATA

ONE THING THAT CAN PREVENT THE gathering of data that's crucial to identifying waste and its causes is the use of a blocked column in a team's workflow. In the resistance chapter, we experienced resistance from Ruth, the Scrum Master, to moving away from the blocked column. Now we'll turn our attention to capturing data on waste, deciding on a system of measurement, and integrating this system with everyday work patterns.

Having taken the first step successfully with Ruth's team, the work that had been started was now visible rather than being hidden in plain sight. The next step was to collect data about the work items and their progress. Each evening we went to the teams' physical boards, took a photo and built a time-lapse view that helped us reflect on how items on the board were changing (or not). Over time, it was obvious that in every team there were alarming numbers of blocked tickets, all part of the work-in-progress (WIP) but not actively being worked on. It was vital that we understood why each blocked work item was not progressing, and this led to the next conversation with Ruth.

Us: "Ruth, can you ask the members of your feature team to start adding some blocked data by flagging in Jira when the work can't progress?"

Ruth: "What shall I ask them to put in the tickets?"

Us: "Ask them to drop some thoughts in. As a lab, team and tribe, we should be able to obtain enough knowledge collectively to learn from, and then act to remove, the waste."

Flagging a work item is straightforward. In software tools such as Jira, users can set a ticket to 'flagged'. This setting of a flag indicates and records that the work item has been blocked, rather than moving the ticket to a blocked column.

Once the Jira ticket has been flagged, it is clearly visible on the board as the ticket changes colour and is shown as orange. This is a clear indicator to all those in the team, lab and tribes associated with the work that there is a problem preventing the ticket from being actively worked on, and therefore progressed. Keeping blocked work in the state where it has been blocked provides the underlying data needed to build the knowledge of flow. This ensures that:

- The total amount of work-in-progress (WIP) does not increase.
- The blockage is visible and clear to the team each day and provides a focus to remove the impediment that is affecting the work of the team, lab and tribe.
- A date stamp is created at the point when a blockage is identified; flagging a Jira ticket sets a start date that is recorded in the Jira dataset.

Although we have used Jira to highlight the approach, many alternatives to Jira also have flagging functionality. Even if you are working from paper or a whiteboard, the approach can be applied simply by a visible marker being placed on the card, ticket or sticky note, so that it remains in the workflow state where the blockage has occurred. The same concepts and methods detailed below can then be applied to determine the impact and consequences that blockages and waste are having on your organisation.

Teams starting out in Agile typically set themselves up with a workflow that includes a blocked column. Typically, this is on a whiteboard but it can then become the de facto Jira workflow. This creates bad habits for working as a team or a lab from day one because work that is blocked is moved into that status. This work will be talked about at the daily stand-up by the development team as more work is pulled into the 'doing' or in-progress column.

The behaviours this creates in the lab and feature team, which then stick, are as follows:

- When work is blocked, it is moved to a new status. This means the teams lose track of time in a particular status.
- By not knowing how long a piece of work remains in each status, the labs and teams cannot truly measure cycle time in progress.
- Moving work into 'blocked' results in more work coming into 'doing', thus increasing work-in-progress (WIP).

A cleaner state is to set up your labs and feature teams with no blocked columns (Figure 5.1). When work is blocked on a whiteboard with this workflow, teams can put a red dot or sticker on the ticket and write the date work was blocked and a reason. In a software tool such as Jira, teams and labs can use out-of-the-box functionality as detailed above: they right-click and "Add flag and comments" to the Jira ticket.

Figure 5.1 Visualise the work with no blocked column

Doing it this way creates positive lab and team behaviours from day one:

- When work is blocked it stays where it is and the cycle time of the workflow status can be measured.
- Work-in-progress is not increased as the lab and teams should focus on resolving blocked work, rather than pulling in other, less valuable work.

One month on, we arranged to review the data from Jira with an analyst, the lab Product Owner and Ruth (Scrum Master). It's fair to say that this was an underwhelming experience! The data did not provide any of the insight we were expecting and certainly no actionable information and knowledge. We had assumed that, with the ability to record what was happening in relation to blocked work, team members would do just that. How wrong we were!

For years, team members had been putting tickets into a blocked column or status. Now, they were flagging blocked items as we'd requested. But to describe the impediment and reason for the blockage, they were simply writing 'blocked', or in some instances using no text description at all. We could see the number of blockages and the cumulative number of days that work items had been blocked (already numbering in the hundreds), but we had no information on which to act.

What we had experienced was an echo of a management approach and logic dating back to the nineteenth century. By the turn of that century, Frederick Winslow Taylor was world-renowned for his innovative approach of applying the scientific method to organisational improvement. His book describes not only his approach, but also the conditions required for the application of his method.[1] One of these essentially places improvement as a pursuit that is solely for managers. The role of the workers was to undertake the work; the role of the managers was to plan and improve the work.

Due to the physical and manual work typical of that time, Taylor was able to observe all labour, measuring all that was necessary to give him a detailed understanding of the activity and the work. He then used detailed specifications of the activity and how the tasks should be completed, which allowed him to tune the work to peak efficiency. Putting in controls ensured that multiple workers would follow the same specified standards and processes, thereby ensuring efficiency at scale. Aping the scientific fashion of the era, Taylor had essentially created clockwork factories.

The performance data and results were inarguable. His approach, and the assumptions he had of those that did the work, could be challenged, however. Today, some of his statements are not only known to be inaccurate but are also considered unpleasant and offensive. Within his clockwork factory, he had reduced human beings to mere components in a machine.

In his book *Team of Teams*, General Stanley McChrystal gives an excellent summary of Taylor, the emergence of his doctrine and its limitations when applied to complex problems, such as knowledge work.[2] In addition to General McChrystal's book, there is a growing body of work that describes the importance of teams having autonomy and being able to self-organise when operating in complex domains or problems. This decentralisation of knowledge and decision-making is important for organisations when engaging with data and measures. If done correctly, it provides a true understanding of performance and the ability to spot and respond rapidly to changing conditions and circumstances.

If knowledge is not decentralised, data is merely raw material for traditional management information or key performance indicators. These are then rolled up the levels of hierarchy until managers at the correct level of authority can review and decide on action. This mirrors Taylor's approach without the advantage that Taylor had of being able to relate the data he viewed with his own observations.

In John Seddon's work, the questions of what data to use, why it is being used and how it should be used are described by three principles.[3]

PRINCIPLE 1: THE TEST OF A GOOD MEASURE

The test of a good measure is: *does this help in understanding, learning and improving performance*? Management information or key performance indicators are often used as levers of control by senior management. The activity of teams is reported and the data and measures in these reports are then used by managers to make decisions. Decisions such as how much work teams should undertake without knowledge (such as the different types of work, hidden work and the capacity of the teams) are often the cause of the teams having too much work-in-progress.

Another prevalent example of data and measures being used in the wrong way is when changes are made to the process or Lean Value Stream. Traditional management often has a preoccupation with costs and this can lead to decisions about batching work when other teams and organisations are required to complete activity. An example of this is penetration testing. Rather than engaging and paying for a team to conduct the testing once a week, the work instead is batched together and conducted once a month.

The reduced impact on cost is referred to as 'economy of scale'. However, the change in process introduces a queue that impacts the flow of the work. This is accepted as part of the process and therefore is rarely challenged as a blockage. If an item of work is not being actively worked on then the work is being blocked, even if the process causing the blockage is working exactly as intended. If it looks like a pig, sounds like a pig and smells like a pig, then it probably is a pig.

PRINCIPLE 2: MEASURES MUST RELATE TO PURPOSE

The purpose of an organisation or a department is why it exists or is needed by customers or other departments in the organisation. For example, the purpose of a health service is to make people better or stop them from being unwell. Of course, there are things that matter about *how* that purpose is met from the patients' perspective, i.e. length of wait and a treatment that doesn't cause further complications or prevents the issue from recurring.

How clear is your organisation, department or team about its purpose? If they are not clear, how can you evaluate the measures you currently have? Identify what you need and don't currently have. Taking a step back and engaging teams in a discussion about purpose can be profound and powerful. However, it can also be a challenging exercise to define just what it is that the team is there for. Easier Inc's blog on this topic gives great insight into how to do this in practice.[4]

PRINCIPLE 3: MEASURES MUST BE INTEGRATED WITH THE WORK

In this principle, 'the work' is the activity that happens so that the team, department and organisation can meet their purpose. This principle reflects where the locus of control lies in the organisation. If the data and measures are aggregated into reports and fed up the line to managers, the locus of control lies with the managers. If the measures are in the hands of those that do the work, so that decision-making and learning are in proximity to the work, the locus of control is with the teams. That leaves the managers with a different locus of control, which is over strategy, direction and alignment of the organisation.

With these principles in mind, let's return to the situation we faced with Scrum Master Ruth and her team. We had implemented the flagging mechanism with the team but they weren't returning any actionable information. This behaviour and output were unintended but, in hindsight, we should have expected it. Trying to move an organisation that is blind to waste to one in which waste is visible is a complex problem. Progress can only be made through experimenting and learning.

Ruth and I looked again at the data and discussed the outcome that we thought we needed from the team. We then identified the need to improve the commentary in the flagging of blocked data by capturing some key information. This work was taken forward via an experiment, with the belief that the teams would benefit from an improved waste data set.

The template was incorporated into the team's Jira project. On identifying that a work item was blocked by right-clicking the Jira ticket and flagging, a prompt was given to comment on the blockage and provide three key bits of information:

- **Who** - The team or element of the organisation that is blocking the work.
- **Why** - Why the ticket is blocked.
- **Impact** - The impact of that piece of work being blocked.

Table 5.1 below shows an example of a flagged ticket with these three bits of information.

WHO	Supplier XYZ Digital Systems
WHY	The supplier has failed to supply the company ABC for user story or task which is preventing Feature Team AAAA from delivering the AAAAA MI report to Customer ABCD.
IMPACT	Customer ABCD needs this MI report in order to complete a report to the external regulator. Customer ABCD will not be able to trade and sell product AAAA until the MI report is received and signed off by the external regulator.

Table 5.1 Example of a flagged ticket

A month later and the experiment had provided a much-improved set of data. We were starting to see the teams, companies and individuals that were delaying the progress of work items. It was still not perfect. The experiment had resulted in a prototype that was only being used by a team. Our view was indicative of what was happening across the organisation but we had no way of knowing whether this was representative or actionable. It was the tip of the iceberg.

EXERCISE: WASTE DATA MEASURES

Go to your departments and teams and ask them to comment on the causes of blocked work, utilising both the team members and Scrum Masters. Ask them what the main constraints are that affect value delivery to the customer and what impact that is having on the organisation. Do not be surprised if they are unable to answer your questions. You should split the exercise into two parts:

Part 1

Ask them to identify the most recently blocked work item, share the template described above, and ask them to complete the template for the blocked work item. This will help you learn whether the template we used is suitable for your organisation and what difficulties or challenges your teams might encounter when capturing the all-important data required for identifying waste that is disrupting the flow.

Part 2

Next, ask them:

a) What data and metrics they routinely look at. This might be story points started and finished, sprint velocity, or how much capacity they have.

b) What data and metrics are used outside of the team about their performance, i.e. what MI or KPIs have a view of their performance and what is being measured. This might include the run cost of the team, the number of work items completed in a reporting period, or risks open against the team.

Having gathered a view of the data and metrics being used inside and outside the team, run these against John Seddon's measurement principles. For each metric, consider:

- Does it relate to the purpose of the team/department/organisation?
- Does it provide insight into a characteristic that matters to a customer or user of the products being created?

- What is it being used for? Is it merely an organisational control or is the team able to describe how they use it to learn and improve the way they work?
- Who is using it? Is it being used by those that actually do the work?

Part 2 of this exercise will tell you the size of the challenge. You might already have identified that your organisation/department/team does not have the right metrics or they may not be using metrics for the right reasons. Plus, changes required in the organisation may not merely lie in the feature and product teams but in all areas, including the management functions.

LEARNING AT SCALE

Having learned about the prototype in just one team, there was now a need to experiment and learn at scale. We had insight from one team amongst many others. We anticipated that we would meet the same sort of resistance from many other teams as we had when first introducing the idea to Ruth's team. So we decided that the first move should be to engage other teams in the lab in which Ruth's team belonged.

The product owner and I again opted for the coffee-and-cake approach to engaging more teams. Once again the enticement worked, and we provided an overview and a briefing, starting with the why, what and where the organisation hoped to get to. Nonetheless, it still generated a lot of difficult questions from the crowd. Our answers did seem to satisfy those posing the questions and the audience seemed comfortable with the approach. But at this stage, we weren't completely sure if it was the cake or the presentation that had made the proposition amenable. Still, at least we could now start experiments with a larger number of teams.

Six months later, our data was still patchy and incomplete and not all the individuals that had attended the briefing were flagging blockages to our liking. On the plus side, there was now more data and we had more learning. The lab and its teams had produced a Pareto chart to visualise waste. However, this had required a fair amount of manual interpretation of the text to generate the themes and classification. We'd intended that the teams group and classify the data themselves but since this did not generate the expected output, we generated the themes ourselves as an interim measure.

What we learnt from this experience is that the flagging mechanism is really only a tool. It may be a necessity for visualising the waste, but it is not sufficient in and of itself. (As the Agile Manifesto sets out: individuals and interactions over processes and tools). The feature teams struggled as the individuals and feature team collectively didn't have experience with using data. That meant they didn't have the capability to develop the information and insight necessary to take improvement action. In later chapters, we'll discuss the classification and theming of data and look at techniques to remove the waste and measure the impact of doing so.

The journey of working with teams and the organisation to start capturing waste and getting meaningful data to act on is difficult. The events described in this chapter took place over 12 months, and we met resistance every step of the way. Durability and the will to succeed in improving your organisation is key.

But it is worth the journey. When resistance decreases, the curiosity in the organisation increases along with the awareness that action needs to be taken to remove waste from the system. In the next chapter, we'll look at the impact of the data on waste you've collected so far.

TAKEAWAYS

⇨ Waste blocked work increases the lead time to deliver meaningful products to the customer.

⇨ Waste blocked work can create further waste in the lab/teams which can slow the delivery of meaningful products to the customer.

⇨ Obtaining good data and making this sustainable will take time and persistence.

⇨ Obtaining waste data will increase frustration as teams see the organisational problems.

CHAPTER 6

SENSING WASTE AND ITS IMPACT

IMAGINE THAT YOU HAVE COMPLETED A job interview in which you were sold the idea that you will be joining an amazing organisation with teams delivering meaningful products at pace. When you arrive in the role, you expect to see the equivalent of a sleek speedboat functioning smoothly and flying through the water. But instead you find a boat that hasn't been maintained for years. It is covered in barnacles, each slowing the boat as it tries to make its way through the water, at times forcing it to come to a complete stop.

Sticking with our boat analogy, the solution to this problem begins with identifying the barnacles. You'll need to gather information to locate where they are on the boat and understand their impact on the boat's ability to move through the water. Removal of each barnacle will improve your boat's ability to glide through the water. It will achieve higher speeds more sustainably, using less fuel. This is the equivalent of faster delivery of meaningful products to your customers, using less capacity and therefore delivering more for the same investment budget.

By following our approach so far, as CTO you have identified that there is waste in your organisation—something that might have been new to you. Now you're at the stage where curiosity is building and so the next question becomes: exactly what information is needed to remove waste and improve software delivery?

Our experienced Scrum Master, Ruth, was already on the journey with us and willing to try new ideas. However, we were fully aware that 'telling' people what to do leads to reduced investment by those being told, lowering motivation and engagement. We therefore need to be truly adaptive and bring the organisation with us, encouraging experimentation and unconstrained thinking.

In this chapter, we'll show you some of the techniques we have developed and used successfully to find and capture waste information at team level and demonstrate how this information can be scaled up. This will provide insight into the most common and disruptive causes of waste that are slowing the pace of flow in your organisation, as well as their consequences for economic performance.

TEAMS, LABS AND TRIBES

As a CTO, you typically enable transformational change via teams operating in structures such as labs or tribes, perhaps with component teams or release teams. If your organisation is established, these teams will have been running for some time, albeit under different names and structures. Organisations grow accustomed to maintaining them. They spend millions each year keeping existing products and services running, as well as trying to adapt, develop and deliver the most meaningful products possible.

The transformation focus in established organisations is often on the team structures, establishing new roles such as Product Owners, Scrum Masters and dev team members. The transformation will include methods of change, which quickly start to bear fruit as work becomes visible on physical boards and virtual boards. However, as we explored in a previous chapter, while work may be visible it doesn't mean it's flowing effectively. Waste causes constraints that prevent or delay essential activity (labelled 'value work') being delivered to your customers.

Waste is well recognised in service organisations, despite it being more difficult to observe, track and measure there than in manufacturing settings. Waste attracts such focus not only because it causes delays but because it impacts the effort expended in organisations. John Seddon recognised this through a simple but profound relationship:

Capacity = Value Work + Waste

Capacity in this case is the resource available in a process or system to produce or serve a required outcome. For example, a production line in an automotive factory requires materials, parts, machines and people to produce vehicles that are desired and purchased by customers. The materials, parts, machines and people are the capacity. These will be engaged in assembling the vehicle or else they are not active (waste) or are active on avoidable activity, such as resolving quality issues (also waste).

In the case of service systems, when a customer has requested a service but does not get it, they will often engage with the provider again and again until they do. An example is when you order a new broadband package. Traditionally, that re-engagement has been through telephone calls to call centres. Listening to those incoming calls naturally reveals that customers are disappointed, frustrated and sometimes angry. Call handlers find these calls difficult and frustrating, as invariably they have not been involved in previous activity to provide the service. They are not personally installing cables and routers.

John Seddon called this re-engagement by customers Failure Demand and identified that this not only affected customer satisfaction but also the cost of provision.[1] When Failure Demand occurs, there is often duplicated activity and re-work in response. The organisation provides customers with what they are due, as well as taking calls from customers that the organisation does not need (or want) to receive ('Failure Demand'). In other words, Failure Demand is where customers don't want to make these calls in the first place—a lose/lose situation for all parties involved!

Dealing with Failure Demand therefore requires capacity from the process or system. It is a transaction with the customer that is both unwanted and preventable. By John Seddon's definition, it's a failure to do something right from the customer's perspective. Any capacity used to deal with Failure Demand is therefore waste, as visualised in Figure 6.1 below.

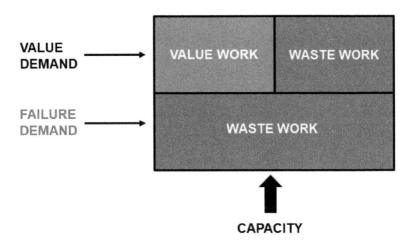

Figure 6.1 Capacity used to deal with Failure Demand is wasted

Given the old adage that time is money, we can think about the capacity for work either as the amount of time that the resources in a process or system can be running productively, or the money that it takes to run those resources. In traditional organisations, money, or more specifically costs, often get a great deal of focus. Helping others in an organisation understand the financial impact of blockers, impediments and delays in the processes and systems can provide a collective focus and understanding of the waste, and the impact of wasted capacity.

Returning to the context of software development, the effective use of resources is clearly an important concern to CTOs. It can be sensed through flow, particularly some of the flow metrics outlined by Mik Kersten in his book *Project to Product*:

- Flow Time.
- Flow velocity (throughput).
- Flow efficiency.

Other metrics that help sense how well the resource is being used are:

- Number of defects.
- Amount of rejected work
- Amount of work-in-progress (WIP) that has been neglected.

Defects are the software development equivalent of Failure Demand. If the code is developed and tested as intended, there will be no defects. When a defect occurs, it is unexpected and demands attention, just as Failure Demand does in service organisations.

Rejected work refers to items that have been started but development has stopped and a decision was taken that the feature was no longer required. In the early stages of product development, such as the ideate, design, or test and learn stages, this may be a 'good' rejection; it may be the epitome of the 'fail fast' mantra. However, work rejected in the later stages of the workflow, such as the Route to Live or release backlog, may be a 'bad' rejection. Here, the decision to reject may have been driven by factors unrelated to the efficacy of the product. When studying the amount of rejected work, it is also important to know the stage at which items were rejected in order to ascertain whether it was a good or a bad rejection.

Neglected WIP is a feature where work has started but is not complete. Capacity has been invested in the feature but in its partly completed state, it is of no value to the customer or the organisation. It is worth noting that traditional accountancy approaches in manufacturing consider partly completed items (i.e. WIP) as inventory and WIP is therefore treated as an asset on the balance sheet. However, it is difficult to see how partly developed or tested code could be considered as an asset.

In addition to organisational and permanent metrics, you could also study what is happening for individuals. Whenever their time is 'wasted', capacity is also wasted. Quantifying time spent by individuals on the activities below provides further insights:

- Unnecessary effort to find information, access resources, access expertise or obtain approval.
- Dependencies: either being interrupted by someone that requires help, or requesting and chasing when dependent on someone else.
- Duplicated effort to provide other parts of the organisation with the same information.
- Cognitive overhead when context-switching due to conflicting priorities or WIP.

These may well be regularly experienced by many in the organisation but their occurrence is often invisible.[2] When teams are using the blocked column, these disruptors to individuals are rarely seen. The challenge, therefore, is again to make waste visible through data. Some teams visualise work on physical boards using cards; others use Agile software tools. Some may use both.

Even without detailed data, you can still approximate the effects of waste to sense its impact, particularly on financial performance. One way of approaching this is to focus on income/revenue to get an idea of the cost of delay.[3] Of course, the expected revenue that comes from a completed feature, product or project is only anticipated, not certain! So rather than revenue/income, you could instead focus on the impact on the cost of running the organisation, or more specifically the production system. Before exploring this in the software development context, let's take a look at learning that's been gained from service delivery, specifically call centres.

John Seddon cites Failure Demand in call centres to be between 40-60% of the work that operators undertake. So what impact does this have on their economic performance? As Failure Demand is preventable, all the activity in response to it is therefore waste. For a simple, albeit conservative, view, let's make three assumptions:

1. The activity and effort to respond to a Value Demand matches the response to a Failure Demand.
2. The system responds perfectly to Value Demand, therefore there's no waste.
3. Failure Demand remains predictable at 40% of all the calls taken by operators in the call centre.

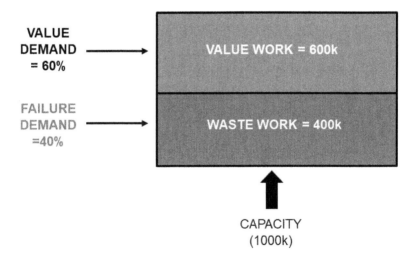

Figure 6.2 The cost of waste due to Failure Demand

For illustration, if the call centre costs one million (insert currency of choice!), then the impact of the Failure Demand on waste activity is four hundred thousand (Figure 6.2). In other words, when seen through the lens of customers, 40% of the calls are preventable. This is rather different from the common assumptions that more operators are required to deal with long wait times, or that operators are spending too long on calls. The diagnosis changes from the system not having enough capacity to identify what's really causing the Failure Demand.

Switching back to software development, Value Demand equates to the features, as well as the risk mitigation required to maintain quality characteristics such as security or adhering to new regulatory requirements.[4] Failure Demand occurs when the system fails to do something, or do it correctly. In this context, service incidents occur as unintended consequences of recent changes or where there is an underlying issue, often described as technical debt. Understanding how much activity and time is spent dealing with incidents provides our first insight into waste.

Capacity in the end-to-end software delivery system may not simply be in the feature team alone. Activity may occur before the feature team commits to the work, such as researching, shaping, selecting and prioritising. Teams may also not have the ability to 'release on demand'. Once they have completed their activity the item is in a state of 'done' from their perspective, but it is not 'done' from the perspective of customers or users.[5] Capacity is also needed after the feature team has finished to ship or release the feature. This may include sign-off, approvals, further testing, integration and other related activities in the Route to Live.

If activity is spread across multiple teams in the Value Stream, you face the challenge of knowing where the waste exists in the multiple teams, labs, and tribes.[6] Without this knowledge, you will not be able to sense its impact, nor will the organisation be able to experiment and remove the waste to increase capacity and the value flowing to customers. In order to sense the waste, we need a mechanism to visualise the activity, which we can then overlay with data about the waste.

VISIBILITY AND IMPACT

Value Stream mapping is a lean technique that lends itself well to making the intangible work of software delivery visible. According to software company Kanbanize, "A Value Stream map displays all the important steps of your work process necessary to deliver value from start to finish. It allows you to visualise every task that your team works on.[7] However, unless all the work and tasks in the Value Stream are completed in one team, activity must be mapped across multiple teams. As CTO, the advantage you have is your mobility and access within the organisation. The disadvantage is that you aren't close to the detail of how teams work and the processes they have to follow. Therefore, you'll need to lead a group of participants from the various teams involved in a collective, participative exercise.

There are many ways to conduct this exercise and plenty of guidance on approaches, some of which even take into account the geographical spread and separation of teams and home working arrangements. The key output is an artefact that identifies waste. It displays the activity that accounts for how an idea, opportunity or problem is understood and how the solution is designed, developed, tested, deployed, and ultimately evaluated as a product or service. It should be understandable and usable, so a balance needs to be struck between too much detail (down to each keystroke and mouse movement) and not enough detail, i.e. handovers are missed or work queues hidden. Once the end-to-end activity is visible, the group can discuss where the pain points arise, where the different types of waste occur, and where work joins a queue and waits.

With visibility into the Value Stream, as well as instances where waste occurs, you can then ask the question: So what? More specifically, what is the impact of the identified waste? It is tempting just to think of the impact of waste in terms of capacity, resource or money, i.e. from an efficiency perspective. However, it is just as important to look at effectiveness. You might use the words efficiency and effectiveness interchangeably, which is unsurprising as some dictionaries say that the terms are synonymous. But we are using the terms in a very specific way:

- Effectiveness: the quality of being successful in achieving what is wanted.
- Efficiency: a situation in which a person, company, factory, etc. uses resources such as time, materials, or labour well, without wasting any.[8]

A useful distinction is that customers or users are primarily concerned with how effective an organisation is in satisfying their needs, whereas traditional organisations are primarily concerned about efficiency for managing margin and profitability. The fact is that the two things are interconnected and being ineffective results in poor efficiency. Failure Demand is a good example of having to deal with additional calls as a result of an ineffective response to customers' original demands. Researchers Modig and Ahlstrom describe this as 'secondary needs', which generate additional work.[9] Being ineffective results in being inefficient. We therefore need to consider the impact of this on the outcomes and performance of the Value Stream from the perspective of the customer/user, as well as on capacity, resources and investment.

WHAT PROVIDES THE INSIGHT?

As blockages occur and are identified, information and insight about the waste is required so that improvements can be made. The key data required about blockages is:

Time (Duration) - The number of days that the work item has been held up (i.e. is waiting and cannot be progressed). Aggregating the number of items that are blocked and the total amount of time for all those items provides you with a sense of the scale of the problem.

Who (Source) - Where in the organisation the source of the blockage originates; this could be a team, a department, a resource or even a role or capability. It may, of course, come from a part of the system that is not in your organisation, i.e. a third party such as a partner or supplier. Again, aggregating blocked items tells you which source is generating the greatest number of instances of waste.

What (Type) - A description of what is preventing the item or feature from progressing and therefore delaying its completion. This may be the need for skills, knowledge or access that sits outside of the team, resource that's not available, or technology that's not working as expected. It may be waiting for approval or another team to complete the activity. There are many different types of blockages.

Impact (Effect) - Understanding the impact of an item or feature being held up is important to highlight the damage being done to performance, strategy, vision, and ultimately the organisation's survival. Not all items are equal in the value they create. A story to add a minor enhancement to an existing product does not hold the same value as a story that's an essential part of a new product. Without the story completing, the product cannot be released. Impact data helps sense things like 'cost of delay' in addition to the effect explored in earlier chapters that blocked work has on work-in-progress'(WIP), context switching and time to complete.[10]

In Table 6.1 below are examples of insight data, using a scenario of a snapshot in time where the current date is 1st September:

Time (Duration)	Who (Source)	What (Type)	Impact (Effect)
Started: 10 July Ended: 3 Aug Duration: 24 days	Cyber security team (internal)	Waiting for penetration testing to be completed	User story linked to epic providing new customer functionality. Expected to reduce customer call Failure Demand by 12%, equates to 2.3 full-time employees (FTE) effort per day.
Started: 20 Aug Ended: 15 Sept Duration: 26 days	Third-party software supplier (external)	Software security patch	New product cannot be launched with access for 100 internal users due to security. Business carries a risk of having to use unsupported, out of date software until the security patch is solved. Feature team of 10 persons is unable to complete the value release to internal customers. Impacts: 26 days where the security was vulnerable to the customers. 26 days where the whole team had to context switch. 26 days where the most valuable piece of work in terms of value could not be progressed.

| Started: 10 July
Ended: 18 July
Duration: 8 days | Governance team (internal) | Design approval | Story linked to epic, providing design sign-off for go live.
Design could not be processed.
Expected to improve the accuracy of the customer data and offer enhanced customer terms on interest rate.
Impacts:
8 days where design was not being worked on.
8 days where the whole team had to context switch.
8 days where the most valuable piece of work in terms of value could not be progressed. |

Table 6.1 Examples of insight data

Later in the book, we will explore how to take the base data of individual blockers from a variety of teams to draw out the themes and common causes having the biggest impact.

GETTING THE DATA

Having established what data is needed and why, the challenge is how to get it and make the work visible. If cards or tickets on the board do not reflect reality, i.e. work is missing or items aren't in the correct workflow state, the work is still not visible.

Assuming that the prerequisite has indeed been met, the options below are for teams working with both physical boards and those using software tools. You will need to work with a select number of teams first before scaling up and drawing data across all the teams in the organisation.

TEAMS USING PHYSICAL BOARDS AND NO SOFTWARE TOOLS

These teams typically visualise their work on a board displaying the different workflow states. The work is visualised with physical cards or even sticky notes to capture user stories and epics. They often allocate an estimate of effort or sizing. The cards may include an estimate of the number of hours or story points allocated, or a relative sizing mechanism. For example, T-shirt sizing is a method for teams to size user stories by considering each user story against its respective T-shirt size, as shown in Figure 6.3.

Figure 6.3 T-shirt sizing

The first check to make is how the team deals with work that is blocked. If it is not completed in a sprint, there may be a routine 'carry forward' into the next sprint, without ever registering and recording the issues that prevented the work being completed as planned. Where teams use story points, you may find that if a story cannot be completed in the sprint, it is split so that part of the story can be shown as completed in the sprint. The remaining part appears as a new story in the next sprint. Again, the causes and issues that prevented the work completing in sprint are invisible and lost.

The most common mode of working employed by teams is to use a 'parking lot' or blocked column. We discussed previously why blocked columns are disruptive when optimising flow. With work-in-progress (WIP) increasing, items stall and age, and time to market deteriorates. In order to gather data with the team, the first intervention needs to address the use of blocked columns. Teams need a simple visual mechanism to signal that work is blocked, as discussed previously in the chapter on flagging waste data.

The sticky note signalling the blockage on a physical board provides a mechanism to capture data. For each blockage, the team can capture the following information:

- **Blocked start date:** Date that the work item (epic, story, task) is blocked.
- **Who:** Source or origin of the blocker.
- **What (Type):** Thing that is preventing progress.
- **Impact:** Effect the blocker is having.
- **Blocked end date:** Date the work item is unblocked.

A growing collection of sticky notes signalling blockers on the board or in an envelope does not provide any information—the data on each sticky note still needs to be collated and consolidated. The easiest approach is to use a spreadsheet, which will also enable analysis. Over time, this can be collated with information from other teams so that a picture can be built of waste throughout the organisation.

TEAMS USING AGILE TECHNOLOGY

For teams using Agile software or applications, there are usually functions to tag or label work items, which would provide the necessary visibility of which stories are blocked. In some cases, the software already has a specific mechanism for marking a work item as blocked. Jira is an example of this.[11] In Jira, when a ticket has been flagged to indicate that it has been blocked, it is clearly visible by a colour change to orange.

Another common feature of Agile software is that work items are time-stamped to recognise events such as work items passing a team's commit point or the completion of the work. You can utilise this functionality to gather data that teams working with physical boards gather manually.

The Start and End of work being blocked can be captured from the time stamps for the events of work being flagged as blocked. The number of days blocked can then easily be calculated.

For the **Who, What (Type)** and **Impact** data, explore the comments options that come with the flagged, tagging and labelling functions. Have the team identify and test approaches to exploiting the software functionality and capturing the Who, What (Type) and Impact data. As the team explores the functionality and the instances of blockers, it builds the common themes and grouping of waste. This may allow picklist options to be built in, which will help other teams use the approach and allow data gathering at scale.

At this point, it is worth noting a health warning: using software and electronic tools can take far more time than running a physical board with manual data capture. There is also a risk that teams become preoccupied with the tooling and how it can be used rather than the real problem at hand: understanding and removing waste from the organisation.

EXERCISE: OBTAIN WASTE DATA KNOWLEDGE

Task a number of teams and gather the key data (Time, Who, What, Impact) using the manual approach with a physical board. Stay close to this work and help the teams involved to reflect and review what has been learnt. The key things they need to understand are:

- How well does the approach work for the team?
- What has been learnt about the delays that impact the team's work?
- What stage in the workflow are the delays occurring?
- What is the source of the blockers?
- What impact are they having?
- What would the team want you, as CTO, to focus on and help them with?

This approach ensures that you are connected directly to what the teams are doing and learning. In other words, you are not getting filtered interpretations of what's happened and what's needed for improvement. This is a key enabler for leaders to understand, learn and take action based on knowledge and personal insight.

EXERCISE: GROUP WASTE DATA

With a group of your leaders, review what happened with the teams and ask the group to reflect on how this new understanding and information could be used with key stakeholders, such as:

- Third parties and suppliers.
- Product Owner communities.
- Scrum Master Communities.
- Engineering communities.

- Finance functions.
- Executives on the board.

The objective is to get all key parties to understand the scale of the problem that waste is having by being in the work and obtaining the knowledge of the scale and impact themselves. As a CTO, you need to generate urgency to act on the waste. You want those around you on this transformational journey to have that "Oh sh*t moment". By getting everyone to that point, you might be able to provide leverage, support and collaboration to help you remove waste and increase capacity.

GO TO THE SOURCE

Building information that enables you to act effectively is key, no matter how far your organisation is along in its transformation journey, or its technical capability. Capturing specific data manually or electronically is required to understand the impact of waste. No matter the approach, it routinely requires input and insight from teams completing the work. It also requires leadership to ensure that effective action happens through the use of the data and insights from teams. In the words of the Japanese business pioneer Taiichi Ohno: "Genchi Genbutsu!" ("Go to the source!". In the next chapter, we'll explore how you can collate and build on data collection to identify the top blockers.

TAKEAWAYS

Teams, tribes and labs:

⇨ Can capture and make waste visible without Jira if needed.

⇨ Will quickly be able to sense and visualise where their waste problems are.

⇨ Will understand what is slowing them down and grow curious about resolving problems.

CHAPTER 7

IDENTIFYING TOP BLOCKERS

YOU MAY HAVE TENS OR EVEN thousands of teams following adaptive Agile frameworks and applying Kanban, Scrum or any of the other Agile methods. Teams have therefore been empowered to break down work into manageable pieces that deliver beneficial outcomes to customers and users. The teams will no doubt experience work being blocked and will individually look to manage and address the blockers that prevent them from completing their work.

However, if all teams in the organisation are experiencing work being blocked due to various causes, but multiple teams are experiencing the same causes, there is an opportunity to address blockers that are impacting work in multiple teams. Each team may be unaware that many other teams are encountering the same issues they are.

In addition to the blockers experienced within teams, we should consider what is happening to the progress of features flowing through the entire system. Unless teams can deploy their completed work into production and therefore release it on demand, it is very likely that work developed by a team will have to be passed on to other teams in order for it to be released. Completed work that sits in queues waiting for other teams to action is very unlikely to be flagged as blocked by any individual team. It is vital that this queuing and waiting is also framed as blockers if it is disrupting the flow of features, even if the process is working as designed.

In your role as CTO, you will no doubt encounter teams that have work blocked, yet it is very likely that the organisation will still be releasing completed work into production. However, the flow rate of these products to the customers will be slower than it could have been. This is due to the constraints the teams, tribes and labs continually face in the form of waste. By arming your organisation with techniques and capabilities to identify, classify and quantify the blockers affecting your organisation's performance, you will have a view of the most pervasive.

You can then decide which blockers should be the focus of improvement efforts—the big 'barnacles' that prevent flow and sap the energy, motivation and capacity to deliver meaningful products. Earlier in this book, we established techniques to capture waste and blocked information. In this chapter, we will use this information to establish where your improvement efforts should be focused and why.

It is not uncommon for feature teams to have adopted Agile whilst the organisation as a whole has not. This can cause friction in the interactions with different stakeholder groups such as, but not limited to waterfall teams, Project Management Office (PMO) and Audit. They may be using the historic ways of working, with expectations at odds with the Agile practices and mindset that teams are following. One example of this is when stakeholders expect a detailed delivery plan with milestones and Agile teams use a product backlog and continuously deliver in sprints. This causes a misalignment.

In his book, the Agile mindset expert Gil Broza provides an excellent overview of the challenge of the misalignment. He shows how this is rooted in differences in values, and therefore the beliefs that create the principles of the differing perspectives.[1]

Friction between stakeholders and delivery/change teams is clearly problematic, but it is not as harmful as other consequences of misalignment. The traditional mode of management labelled by Deming as 'Command & Control' and also described by Seddon, values tight control, particularly of cost/budget but also risks.[2] It values the experience of individuals, particularly senior decision-makers, so they can use their personal experience for intuitive decision-making. An organisation operating like this is likely to have robust and detailed mechanisms to track financial spend and operational risks.

In this type of organisation, CTOs are typically viewed as performing well if their actual spend matches their forecast spend, have recorded risks and used their experience to mitigate them. If these things are true, a CTO in a traditional organisation will be able to respond effectively to any questions and scrutiny at board level.

Let's now look at this from the perspective of the feature teams. As they hit a problem in a cycle of work, that feature becomes blocked and stops evolving. Using the organisation's risk and issue-management mechanisms, they are likely to log it as required. If it is a risk, it may be escalated and graded in terms of importance. Routine reviews of the risks will be conducted to ensure each one is managed in accordance with its type and importance. This continues until the situation and risk worsens or someone in the organisation sees it as important enough to resolve.

For the affected feature teams, their work remains blocked and other teams potentially encounter the same blocker. Waste accumulates because of the blocked item, and there is a cost of delay to the value created. However, from a risk and finance perspective, the budget and operational risks are being managed and are under control.

In Agile methods, empiricism is a key foundation of how teams operate, using transparency, inspection and adaptation to incrementally achieve the desired outcomes.[3] Feature teams apply empiricism in their development of products. However, traditional mechanisms to manage operational and delivery risk do not apply empiricism. Instead, they use the best judgement available and the completion of actions intended to manage the risk.

An alternative and empirical approach to managing risks is to use real-world observations, as data can then be used to form theories, hypotheses and experiments. These are used to address the issues and blockers in a way that is responsive and timely so that delays are removed, waste reduced and time to market improved. The starting point for this approach is blockers being flagged by individual teams. Understanding more about the effects of the blockers and their impact provides the key information needed for empirical improvement.

DISCOVERING THE COMMON CAUSES AFFECTING A TEAM

Different people can observe similar, or even identical, situations and give differing accounts. Even labels we assign to things can have different meanings or interpretations. For example, an offer of chips to a mixed Anglo-American group will result in quite different expectations of the food they'll receive. We should therefore expect that individuals reporting and recording data about why an item is blocked may do so in very different ways. Equally, the underlying causes of blockers may present in different ways at different times, leading to differences in recording them. Gathering insight into the blockers provides an opportunity to decipher their causes.

By taking the instances of blockers and reviewing the different insights, we can look for things they have in common. One of the easiest ways of doing this is to create a sticky note for each blocker, including how long the blocker has had an impact. Then, place all the blockers on the board and compare the sticky notes, moving them into groups of commonality. These could be common factors in one particular team where there is a dependency, or when a particular capability is not available. The commonality could be related to an environment, a code file or a governance process.

For each grouping of blockers, the impact or the cause can easily be determined by adding up the number of days of impact of all the tickets in that grouping. This clustering activity builds the team's knowledge of the most common and disruptive causes of waste in their Value Stream.[4] One of the ways you can visualise the different causes and their impact is by using a Pareto chart, as shown in Figure 7.1.

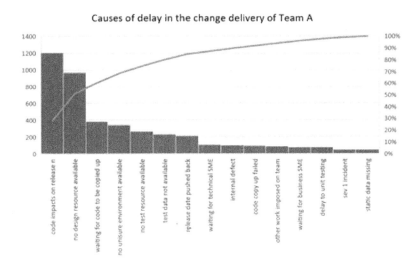

Figure 7.1 Example Pareto chart

Along the x-axis are the different causes of waste that represent a grouping or cluster of blockers; the y-axis shows the cumulative amount of delayed time. Each bar in the chart represents the amount of delay attributed to the cause (i.e. the sum of all the impact of the blockers in the group). The curved line shows the accumulating proportion of delay, so the chart makes visible the cumulative impact the causes have had on all the work completed in that period. The curve begins at the most impactful cause, shown on the left-hand side. In the example, 'code impacts on release n' accounts for almost a third of the overall delay. The last point on the curve encompasses the cumulative effect of all the causes—in other words, 100% of the delay. From this example, we can see that 80% of the impact is down to just five causes. This indicates which causes should be prioritised for problem-solving activity and action to contain their impact or remove them.

THEME AND GROUP DATA

Having the teams, tribes and labs theme the waste data they collect allows them to build a set of base information that can be used to create their Pareto charts, as shown above. Table 7.1 shows how you could work through some of your blocked/waste data and theme it in main categories and subcategories.

Flag description	Flagged time 5 days	Main category	Subcategory
Team A : Governance impact : Delay to Customer X of product release.	12	Governance	Security committee
Team Software Supplier A : Cloud access impact : Delay to Customer X of product release.	5	Software supplier	Supplier ABC
Team B - Governance meeting cancelled due to SME not available to create documents. Now can be represented in 14 days' time to the committee.	10	Governance	Design committee
Team A - Governance meeting cancelled due to SME not available to create documents. Now can be presented in 14 days' time to the committee.	2	Governance	Design committee

Table 7.1 Waste data themed in categories and subcategories

To see how to make sense of the groupings, let's return to the organisation in which we were helping teams learn how to flag blocked work. Creating a Pareto chart moved us a long way towards our objective of reducing waste. With a set of data themed into groups, and the impact of the causes visible, we had a clear view of the main blockers affecting the flow of work in our teams. It was several months into the organisation's journey and we now had information about the time that was being wasted in the Value Stream.

Yet despite the progress and the insights gained, frustration started to appear from the feature teams. We would hear people say: "This data is being flagged by the teams but nothing has happened, no action has been taken to remove it and nothing has happened to make our lives better".

Hearing this can be tough. The scale of the waste affecting your organisation can be shocking, and the organisation has only learnt how to sense it, not to take concerted and meaningful action. It is easy to see this as a negative. But what is really going on? In fact, teams are pulling for leaders in the organisation to take action where the teams cannot. Addressing what is causing teams' frustration will, of course, have the effect of improving flow and increasing throughput and value.

Once the clustering and grouping has been undertaken by more than one team, insight can be synthesised and common causes affecting multiple feature teams in a lab or division can be determined. There may also be benefits in identifying common causes affecting tribes, guilds or communities. As insight is combined from multiple teams, labelling and definition is key, i.e. the label given to a grouping with similarities in one team is consistent with a similarly labelled grouping in another. Once completed, the combination of insight from multiple teams provides a bigger dataset and a closer approximation to the true amount and impact of waste.

DISCOVERING THE COMMON CAUSES AFFECTING THE ORGANISATION

It is insufficient to use insight into blockers from just a few teams. Only data from all teams will provide organisational insight. It will help answer the questions:

- What (by type) and where are the top blockers in the organisation?
- What is the impact in cost, time and delay?

Not only does this highlight where investment and change budget is being wasted, it also provides more empirical insight into operational and delivery risks than any issue and risk log can provide. Just as the work done by a team must be balanced with capacity and therefore prioritised and sequenced, the organisation will not be able to tackle all the causes of blockage immediately and concurrently. There will be a finite capacity available for addressing problems and putting improvements in place. Identifying which blockers are the most pervasive informs prioritisation and the sequence in which their causes are tackled. It's the equivalent of approaching a lake with a fishing rod and being directed by a guide to the exact spot where hundreds of big trout are staked.

Previously, we outlined a method of flagging and capturing instances of waste in teams across the organisation. We're now going to consider how we might derive insight from many more data points from multiple teams at scale to create insight into the common causes of waste. Table 7.2 provides a simple example of data obtained from a number of teams using the flagging method detailed previously. This example is a very small representation of what is likely to be gathered from hundreds, if not thousands, of blockers and delays. Let's consider how we would use such data from a CTO's perspective, and what insight would provide useful and actionable information.

Non-productive time (Days)	Who	What (Type)	Impact
10	Third-party – Company A	Resources not ready.	Product launch date delay, impact on customers, brand reputational damage, impact on revenue.
5	Governance – Policy B	Governance committee only sits once a month.	Delaying release of work items.
20	Tribe – Team C	Team doesn't have work prioritised to deliver for us.	Product launch date delay, impact on customers, brand reputational damage, impact on revenue
23	Tech – Team D	Access issues not resolved.	Team members cannot start any productive work for the team.
9	Tech – Team D	Need a new password and username.	Team members cannot start any productive work for the team.
20	Third-party – Company A	Resources not ready.	Product launch date delay, impact on customers, brand reputational damage, impact on revenue
8	Tech – Team E	Environment not available.	Delay in completing work items, team pulling in more work and increasing WIP.
15	Third-party – Company F	Resources not ready.	Delay in completing work items, team pulling in more work and increasing WIP.

14	Tech – Team E	Environment not working correctly.	Delay in completing work items, team pulling in more work and increasing WIP.
15	Governance - Policy B	Approval process requires multiple sign-offs	Delay in completing work items, team pulling in more work and increasing WIP. Product launch date delay, impact on customers, brand reputational damage, impact on revenue.

Table 7.2 Example of number of waste Days
by Who / What (Type) / Impact

In this context, non-productive time is not about team members being non-productive; it is the amount of time when the product is not evolving and progressing in its development. Ironically, teams and individuals are rarely inactive or non-productive. There is always something else that can be worked on, which is often described as context switching. As we explored in earlier chapters, this is the common cause of increasing work-in-progress (WIP) and work items ageing as they are neglected.

Even with the simple example above, you no doubt have two questions:

1. How do I group the data to determine the themes and problem statements?
2. How do I determine the impact that the themes are having?

GROUPING

The most obvious grouping of the data is by 'who'; this indicates which parts of the organisation are affecting the overall flow. Typical examples of 'who', or which teams, are causing work to be blocked are:

- Third-party suppliers completing outsourced work.
- Internal teams completing work on behalf of the team.
- Internal teams or third-party suppliers with skills or capability that doesn't exist in the feature team.
- Tech teams that provide environments, data or security access.
- Governance process and application of controls, such as approval boards and forums.

In the example above, there are 10 instances of delay, accounting for a total of 139 non-productive days on the blocked work items. Four of those are identified as being 'tech' and involve two different teams. The total non-productive days from the tech-related blockers is 54. In other words, tech issues account for almost 40% of the non-productive days. If we complete that for the other blockers, we can summarise it in Table 7.3.

Theme	Total days of wait time
Third parties not providing resources at time required	45
Application of Policy B in the organisation's governance	20
Dependency on Tribe C to complete work	20
Tech provision by Teams D & E	54

Table 7.3 Theme of Waste by days lost due to waste

Visualisation of the waste in the lab, team or tribe and to the Product Owner, Scrum Master and development teams is key. But you should also involve teams in the wider organisation as they may not even be aware of the impact that they are having on the transformation journey.

As CTO you may, as many do, have spent time meeting teams and talking to them about their experiences. In these discussions, you may have heard people talk about the impact that other teams have on them and their work. You may even have dismissed this as anecdotal and part of the expected friction between teams. However, the identification and classification of information provides factual confirmation that the problems exist as well as the scale of the problems and their impact on improving performance and customer experience. The problem-solvers in the organisation can then use the themed and categorised waste to target their improvement efforts.

IMPACT

In the example above, the second question related to impact of the waste, which could be considered from a variety of perspectives, such as:

- Costs.
- Delay.
- Reputational damage.
- Impact to customer needs.
- Compliance with regulators.

Just as with backlog prioritisation efforts, determining the most impactful cause of waste is not something that can be done with absolute certainty. Trying to combine several perspectives using historical data, in order to anticipate an impact in the future will always be subjective to some degree. However, addressing any of the key causes will be beneficial, so the assessment of impact is really to identify the causes having the greatest effect. A typical 2x2 matrix as shown in Table 7.4 is one way to visualise and identify the greatest effect and opportunity, with impact on one axis and ease of addressing on the other axis.

High impact	High impact
Difficult to address	Easy to address
Low impact	Low impact
Difficult to address	Easy to address

Table 7.4 Matrix table to visualise waste by Impact and Ease

There are, no doubt, other prioritisation techniques that could be employed. The required effect is simply to establish an order and sequence in which to tackle the causes of waste. This provides you with a mechanism to view waste in all teams and pull together a consolidated view using a consistent method. As Deming stated, "Data are not taken for museum purposes; they are taken as a basis for doing something." This enables you, as a leader, to focus on the things having the greatest detrimental effect.

EXERCISE: CREATING A STORY TO TELL FROM WASTE DATA

Part 1

Pick a feature team or tribe and ensure they have a transformation or change agent to support and challenge them who is also a good problem-solver.

1. Collate some waste (blocked) data, as per Chapter 5 - Flagging data.
2. Theme the data into groups as described in this chapter.

3. Determine the most impactful of the themes, either through the 2x2 matrix described above or some other visualisation and prioritisation mechanism.

4. Using the insight, create a story that you can use to help educate other executives, teams or tribes about the types of waste, their causes, and the consequences for your organisation.

Part 2

When you share the story and insight and encourage others to implement this new way of doing things, be conscious of when and how resistance presents itself. Listen to what people say, how they say it, and their visible reactions. Consider and reflect on their responses to how you shared the story and insight. Different perspectives will resonate with different audiences—each will want to know "what's in it for me?". They will react differently, so listen and learn to continually improve your future communications. This will help increase engagement in the future and better prepare you for future resistance conversations.

INSIGHT FROM THE BOTTOM UP

Scrum Masters and feature teams like to be empowered and try new ways of working, so you'll potentially start to see a multitude of different types of waste classification emerge. Comparing the themes and categorisation as teams start to gather and analyse their data is an important stage in developing an organisation-wide structure for data gathering.

But be aware that well-meaning efforts by central teams to quickly define and impose data-capture mechanisms often results in friction and undermines efforts to encourage local understanding and improvement. Insight should be driven from the bottom up, with categorisation emerging. This then enables organisational patterns to be identified, which point to where improvement efforts should be focused.

TAKEAWAYS

⇨ Teams can get to the main pain point(s) that are creating a reduced pace of flow of products quickly.

⇨ Teams will be curious about the cost and impact of waste, but expect this to take time to grow as a concept.

⇨ Visualise the waste themes.

⇨ Visualise the impact of the delay due to waste in the system.

⇨ Collaborate across teams and Scrum Masters to compare waste data and themes.

CHAPTER 8

PRODUCT OWNERS

WITH THE GROWING POPULARITY OF **S**CRUM as an Agile product development approach, there has been a rapid growth in opportunities to be a Product Owner (PO). However, there's no getting away from the fact that many, though not all, of those in PO roles come from more traditional modes of delivery. They are likely to have experienced a focus on budgets, requirements gathering, and used lots of upfront planning and deliverables as the output. They are also likely to have had, or even been, project or programme managers focused on tracking progress of the delivery versus a plan and the budget. Success involved demonstrating to stakeholders and senior managers that the projects or programmes were on track and on budget.

This rigid focus on a plan can have adverse consequences. Project and programme managers may have been on the receiving end of harsh feedback if their deliveries drifted from the agreed plan and fell into amber or red status. Picture a managerial ticking off in the style of former Manchester United manager, Sir Alex Ferguson, who was famous for giving underperforming footballers the 'hairdryer treatment'.

But while the hairdryer may once have motivated football changing rooms, it's counterproductive in the workplace. Project teams learn to survive by suppressing bad news and covering up any issues with delivery. It was not unusual to find projects reporting all aspects of the delivery as green, while under the surface in the email traffic, it was clear that all was not going to plan. There were often undeclared issues and an ever-increasing risk of budgets being exceeded and completion dates missed.

As Chief Technical Officer (CTO), you will have numerous Product Owners in your organisation, many of whom gained their professional change experience from delivering projects and programmes in a traditional paradigm. In the past, they may well have experienced the hairdryer treatment in response to them being the bearer of bad news. But now we want those same individuals to connect with the work of the teams, exposing the multiple instances and causes of waste in the systems of change for which they are responsible.

To do this, we must ensure the psychological safety of the Product Owners that are expected to operate in the complex domain and deal with uncertainty, volatility and the unexpected. In this chapter, we'll look at the consequences of not establishing psychological safety. We'll see how it affects the ideation, creation and experimentation stages, not to mention gaining knowledge about blockers and the causes of waste.

Product Owners are an important influence on the direction, focus and culture within teams in the Value Stream and the work that flows through it. In this chapter, we will take you through our experience and learning to show how you can work with your Product Owners to achieve the goal of removing waste.

Let's put ourselves in the shoes of Graham, who is a Product Owner in a FinTech environment. From Graham's perspective, we'll reflect on what is required to deliver meaningful products to customers at the rate the market demands. A key element of this is labs, feature teams or tribes gaining knowledge about what matters and is important to customers, and to what extent the solutions and products being developed meet that understanding of the customers and their needs.

Using the received wisdom of the Agile community, the Product Owner role is:[1]

1. Accountable for user stories being in a 'Definition of Ready' state so development teams can immediately start working on them.
2. Accountable, as an owner of the work, for user stories, epics or features to have 'Acceptance Criteria' in place.
3. Prioritises and manages the product backlog.
4. Works closely with business stakeholders to ensure the needs of the customer are understood in relation to the product.
5. Collaborates with the development team(s).
6. Attends the cadences and is aware of what holds the team up in terms of blockers.
7. Tracks progress via a Cone of Uncertainty for the product's journey to release.

A view of a Product Owner, according to Geoff Watts in his book *Product Mastery*, is that a Product Owner is great when they support Agile practices with the following behaviours:

- D - Decisive
- R - Ruthless
- I - Informed
- V - Versatile
- E - Empowering
- N - Negotiable

The most challenging and persistent question a Product Owner frequently faces from business sponsors and key stakeholders is: "When can the new product be released to the market?" This is a completely reasonable question in the digital age, when speed to market and value to the organisation is so important. Even more so is the value to customers, ensuring the product satisfies what the customers want and that they get it when they want it.

To help aid the conversation with the business sponsor or key stakeholder, Product Owners can employ a tool called the 'Cone of Uncertainty'. This allows a conversation based on the flow rates and predictions of progress from the feature teams and labs, based on factual data.

Let's see how this could be useful for our fictional Product Owner, Graham. He has 15 years' experience and is in a large organisation that's moving into the FinTech space. He's worked throughout the organisation, having seen many programmes and projects delivered in the traditional waterfall (linear) way. Delivery to the customer has been slow but this was not recognised by Graham. He finds it normal, based on his previous delivery experience.

Over the past two years, Graham has been coached on Jira, on setting up cadences and prioritising work, and on techniques for developing meaningful products. The product development lab, and teams in the lab, routinely call out to Graham in the daily stand-up in which he participates. He can hear that work is blocked and is able to have a quick discussion about the blockage. However, Graham sees blockages as normal; he neither sees, nor does he ask for, action to remove the causes of the blockages.

His coach has experimented with ways of showing the waste and the impact of the blockers, just as we've outlined in previous chapters. And when Graham is presented with the number of days lost in the delivery of products to customers, he is shocked. Due to blockers and the delays they cause, his lab has lost thousands of delivery days in a single year. (It is very likely that this could be the norm in any organisation with a history in waterfall that moves to Agile working. Typically, organisations are just not set up for an immediate switch to Agile.

The reality for Graham is that his lab and its feature teams do not have the delivery infrastructure, nor do they have effective problem-solving capability. All they have is a mechanism to highlight and track problems upwards through corporate management information (MI) reporting. The skills, capability and desire to remove blockages are all absent. The work is stopped and moved to the blocked column, where it is ignored. Other work is pulled into the system (lab, feature team and/or tribe). As a consequence, the amount of work-in-progress (WIP) increases, context-switching between work items increases, and the rate of delivery of meaningful product to the customer slows.

In the process of making the blockages visible, the teams increase their awareness of the blockers and the impact they are having. But the problem is that this could further increase their frustrations. It's at this point that there is now a risk to the motivation and happiness of individuals in the labs, feature teams or tribes. From their perspective, they are calling out the blockers but no one is dealing with them, so the blockers keep repeating. Understandably, they will start to ask, "Why should we bother calling them out?"

In previous chapters, we've explored the impact that blockages have on capacity and productivity. But we also need to be aware of another impact that blockages have on the organisation's transformation journey. The Agile manifesto and principles have resulted in iterative and emergent approaches to product development. This iterative approach is essentially a series of experiments using scientific method. There are three steps to this. The team frames what they believe is needed (often as a user story). The work is then completed to satisfy that the user story and the team's belief has achieved what was believed. And finally, it's validated using testing and data.

It is this loop of idea to activity to validation of outcome that is critical for dealing with the complexity of creating new products and features. The key to this approach is the speed at which knowledge is gained by moving around the loop. Speed is therefore of the essence, not just for the sake of increased velocity but also for understanding value and whether it is being created for customers and the business.

If teams are continually affected by blockers and the Product Owners are not leading action to remove them and their causes, teams' delivery is slowed. Productivity is affected and you end up with slow feedback loops and slow satisfaction of customer needs. If this happens, market predators, disruptors and competitors will be well placed to out-manoeuvre you.

A Product Owner's first opportunity to sense the issues and the blockers is to connect with how the work is being made visible (see Figure 8.1). If we take Jira as an example, members of the development team flag that an item of their work is blocked. To do this, they right-click on the ticket representing the work item.

Figure 8.1 A Product Owner working via a digital dashboard

The team then makes everyone aware of the flagged item at the daily stand-up, which brings the blockage to the attention of the Scrum

Master. The Scrum Master then makes the Product Owner aware that the work is blocked.

But for those that recognise the importance of improving flow and all the benefits that come from that, sensing the blockages is necessary but insufficient in itself. Let's consider why this is. Within the collective, there are different perspectives and in a typical organisation undertaking a digital transformation these are likely to be:

Product Owner - Assumes everything is okay. Blockages are being logged and the reporting mechanism is in place to report the blockage through the MI.

Scrum Master - Blockages are being reported upwards so the Product Owner is aware. The Scrum Master is probably unaware that they should be taking action to remove the blockers, as this is how the organisation has been set up over many years. It's geared to reporting upwards rather than getting things fixed.

Development team - They are flagging that their work has been blocked. They have no support to remove blockers and see no action from either the Scrum Master or Product Owner. They pull in more work to their system and shift focus (context-switch) to a new piece of work that is not blocked (this may happen many times). Motivation starts to drift as they simply cannot get things delivered and validate whether their solutions are actually achieving the desired outcomes for customers.

Customer - They may or may not be aware that a product is being developed that will provide them with something they want or need. However, they may not have to rely on your organisation. There may well be many other companies that provide a product they want, and those organisations can provide it quicker than yours.

Investor/Shareholder - Other companies are getting the new value products to the customer quicker than your investment and, in turn, you can see the market share reducing. Customers are moving to those who can offer them what they want, when and how they want it!

For new start-ups, blockers will of course occur but it is inconceivable that the blockers would be accepted and ignored. Such lack of action would threaten the very survival of newly formed businesses. Product Owners, early adopter customers, and investors in new commercial ventures do not expect blockers to persist and compromise the delivery of value and commercial benefit. If this is unacceptable to a Product Owner in a start-up, should it be any more acceptable to a Product Owner in a large, established corporation?

If improvement is to happen then learning how to take effective action is imperative. In the previous chapter, we outlined how the blockers and waste can be visualised and the impact understood. For any improvement to happen, these conditions must be in place:

1. Time and capacity are invested to solve the problem.
2. The correct knowledge is applied to the problem.
3. Rigorous problem-solving method is applied.

We'll explore the topic of problem-solving in a later chapter. However, two other conditions are closely connected to the role of the Product Owner. One key element of the role is to provide the feature or development team with a clear view of the priorities relating to the product. It's easy to see how this can be interpreted as a backlog, consisting only of features required to build and enhance products. The reality is that other work has to happen for customers to get value from products and for the products and organisation to remain viable.

Dr Mik Kersten, author of *Project to Product*, outlines how we can think about this work in a simple and all-encompassing way.[1] He describes four flow types that are MECE (Mutually Exclusive and Collectively Exhaustive). They are: features, incidents, risks and debt.

Feature - Business value unit, pulled from the product backlog and then delivered to your customers as a meaningful value product.

Incidents - Problems and incidents caused in the creation of new features, for example, a technical incident that impacts the product released to the customer. This work needs to be completed or it will prevent or slow the feature work from being released to the customers.

Risks - A variety of work can be pulled into work-in-progress (WIP) that has competing demands, such as governance, compliance and more that generate risks to the delivery.

Debts - This is work related to the technical debt that exists in your change system. Unless work is done to remove this technical debt, this could affect the ability to deliver and thus reduce the flow rate of products to your customers.

All of these work types should be made visible and part of the prioritisation, capacity and planning discussions. If not, vital debt and improvement work will be squeezed in, at best, around feature development. Improvement will happen 'off the side of the desk', more than likely through additional hours and effort, potentially leading to burnout and frustration for individuals in the Value Stream. At worst, no improvement activity will happen and blockers will remain in place and continue to affect flow, speed, value, profit and morale.

Product Owners play a key role in assuring the quality and balance of focus and effort across all the flow types. Working with Scrum Masters, they can ensure that all the necessary stakeholder perspectives are brought into the discussions. This provides the opportunity to ensure that no one type of work dominates due to influential or dominant characters advocating its importance.

In many cases, the teams involved in developing products are not able to control all the activity in a Value Stream, from ideation through to deployment to customers. As we explored previously, some of the blockages affecting development teams are outside the control and influence of the teams. Indeed, it's very likely that the knowledge needed to understand and overcome the problem is not in the team. So the Product Owner plays a primary role in helping to resolve what is blocking the team's work. It may involve discussion with leaders and managers in different parts of the organisation to help them understand why some of their resource may be needed.

The information about type, frequency and impact outlined in the previous chapter plays an important part to support the use of resource and capacity in tackling the problem. The information may still need to be augmented by the Product Owner involving other leaders and managers. By bringing them into the team, they will connect to the issue and the blocker themselves. This may even help them understand the capability and expertise necessary to work on the problem.

If the conditions for effective problem-solving are being set and maintained, Product Owners should expect to see problems in different states. Some are waiting to be worked on, some will have seen some progress and, over time, an increasing number will be solved. This is another source of data that helps everyone visualise the progress of improvement efforts. These metrics could be included in teams' cadences, such as the retrospectives and planning events. An accumulation of effective improvement efforts should start to have an impact on flow. Product Owners will be able to use cadences to validate the cumulative effect of improvement activity on common flow metrics such as lead time, throughput and flow efficiency.

DESIRED IMPACT

If you have successfully switched to effective problem-solving that is consistently sensing, identifying and removing blockers and their causes, you will not only expect to see this in the metrics, but also other observable effects too. Let's reflect on the impact and change experienced by the key groups we explored earlier in the chapter:

Development team - Initially, the development team is flagging work as blocked, and the Product Owner and Scrum Master take a keen interest in what is slowing the lab, feature team and/or tribe. The Product Owner is now using metrics and their own experience of connecting to the issues and blockers in the team's work. They are demonstrating true leadership through clearly communicated intent and prioritisation. This has resulted in true alignment throughout the team and with other teams involved in the Value Stream. Dedicated resource and capacity is built into the planning so that blockers are addressed and regular improvement happens through the use of study, data and experimentation.

Product Owner - Now that they are spending time connected with the teams in their work, there is a collective and shared awareness of what is happening and why. There are fewer surprises and crises, while knowledge increases and predictability of delivery improves. Knowledge about what does and doesn't work for customers is increasing and being achieved at a faster rate. Teams are able to achieve more, even with no increase in numbers, resource or working hours.

Scrum Master - Collective insight is being enabled through metrics, and the team is becoming increasingly aligned and self-organised. The Scrum Master role has switched away from facilitating team activity to facilitating action on the system. Now, they focus their efforts on removing blockers from the lab, feature team and/or tribe. Motivation and satisfaction in the team increases, as does the value and recognition of the Scrum Master role.

Development Team - They are flagging work as blocked and are now fully supported to remove waste from the system. They are given time to own and self-fix the problems that exist in their feature team or tribe. They have the confidence that problems that are beyond their control and influence will be picked up and owned by leaders that can.

Customer - Issues they have experienced with products and services seem to be disappearing with increasing speed. They're enjoying new and useful enhancements they hadn't expected but which are really useful.

Investor/Shareholder - Value is being released with increasing pace, there are increasing amounts of features and products on the roadmap, and the organisation is now seen as more competitive in the digital age. The profitability of products and services is increasing, as are the company's overall margins.

Achieving this state is, of course, dependent on many conditions and factors, but the Product Owner has a key role in moving to the desired state. The role is pivotal and influential in setting direction as well as achieving the optimal balance of:

- Delivering quality of service and outcomes today.
- Delivering improved products, service and outcomes tomorrow.
- Improving future delivery of products, service and outcomes.

A Product Owner who is curious, has a growth mindset, and is conscious of their leadership role and impact on collective performance and outcomes, will enable the transformation to the desired state.[2] However, in large organisations that embark on digital transformation, it is common to find programme managers being moved into Product Owner roles. Not only do these individuals need to undertake a learning journey, but the organisation is also changing around them as it transforms.

If they're not proactive, a Product Owner may wait for things to change above and around them before they commit to new ways of working. These Product Owners may consume the time of coaches and Scrum Masters but remain reluctant about acting on new knowledge and adopting new behaviours. This may, of course, be due to an absence of psychological safety.[3] It may also be due to behaviours that persist from their experience of applying waterfall delivery in traditional programme and project management.

As a CTO, you therefore need to select the right individuals to go into Product Owner roles and help those in the role transition to the new values and required behaviours. For those that are unable to adapt, difficult decisions will need to be made. Product Owners that adopt these concepts will bring focus, clarity, alignment and the balance needed to deal with uncertainty and complexity. Being more predictable and operating effectively in complex domains provides these key benefits:[4]

- Predictable time to market of products.
- Predictable costs for product development.
- Increased throughput and flow efficiency (i.e. flow productivity).

The Product Owners help set the tone and operating model of the labs and teams through their leadership and behaviours. Having them on board with your intent, as well as understanding that their own learning and development is key, is crucial. The result will be Product Owners that are clear about the importance of removing the blockers and consequent waste in their product Value Streams.

Even in their transformations to become more adaptive, traditional organisations tend to report waste (blockers) through issue and risk-management mechanisms rather than ownership. To move forward, psychological safety is essential to honest and open conversation, problem-solving, experimentation and a willingness to fail. All of this needs to be enabled by trust and effective leadership, through which self-organising and autonomous teams can develop and succeed.

You can influence Product Owners, giving them the capability to study and act on their own product Value Stream. In the next chapter, we'll explore how leadership influences your mission to reduce waste.

TAKEAWAYS

⇨ Taking the Product Owner with you on the waste journey is key.

⇨ Remove fear for the Product Owner by explaining the benefits at all times.

⇨ Demonstrate to the Product Owner the increase in capacity as a result of reducing waste.

⇨ Bring Product Owners into the work of removing waste and help them understand how their system of change works.

⇨ The hairdryer treatment won't reduce fear; it will inhibit the acquisition of knowledge.

CHAPTER 9

LEADERSHIP INFLUENCE

BY THE LATE **1970**S, THE **E**NGLAND cricket team had a legendary opening batsman in Geoff Boycott, who had scored 100 centuries for his country. His cricketing philosophy was a batting-first approach: score slowly and take as long as you need. The idea was to minimise the risk of getting out and maximise the team's chances of winning. It suited the way cricket was played and how matches were won. But by the mid-to-late 1970s, the game was changing. Teams were scoring more quickly, helped by the introduction of 'all-rounder' players proficient in both bowling and batting.

England's vice-captain, Bob Willis, knew this and effectively overruled his captain Geoff Boycott. To adapt, the whole England team would have to reset its approach and Boycott would need to score more quickly. But Boycott couldn't adapt. After 20-plus years of playing cricket his way, perhaps he was simply too 'hard-wired' to change. So The vice-captain decided to promote Ian Botham, a young allrounder, to bat at No.4. Given strict instructions to run Boycott out in the New Zealand vs England test match of 1978, the result vindicated Willis. England won the match with plenty of time to spare.

How does this relate to you? Well, ask yourself if your organisation seems too hard-wired to change. Sure, management faces a wealth of daily challenges and sometimes it seems that it's enough of a job just keeping the show on the road. There are budget, resourcing, procurement, risk and audit challenges, not to mention the additional activity involved in the transformation. Even with data, information, knowledge and the experience of teams making improvements, many will believe they have more important priorities.

You may have sensed this as resistance and challenge to the notion of improving the delivery of product and change. This is especially true when delivery commitments need to be met and actions completed so that internal processes and requests for status are satisfied. There may have been an expectation that teams undertake this improvement activity, to which managers give their blessing. However, there's an all-too-common belief in many organisations that they are much too busy to be involved in any detail or take any action themselves. Hearing updates on the progress, or more likely the lack of it, is as far as their commitment goes.

In earlier chapters, we explored the imperative of improving flow and the part this plays in adaptation and achieving outcomes that are valued by customers, stakeholders and investors. Sensing the bottlenecks and waste and understanding their causes has become essential. Yet managers are often trapped in an impasse. The pressures and tangible threats of the present often outweigh the unproven and less tangible threats of the future. This chapter will explore this impasse, and what it means to move from a mode of management to one of leadership.

At the heart of this issue is the question of what it means to be a leader. Previously, we touched on a management style that originated in the industrial revolution and proved highly effective in mass manufacturing in the early twentieth century. Organisations were treated as mechanical entities in which standardisation, process and control mechanisms provided predictable outcomes and guaranteed efficiency and productivity. These corporate machines employed workers, who were subject to feelings, emotions, fatigue and other human conditions. This resulted in unwanted variation in organisational performance. The standardisation, process and control mechanisms were also highly effective in managing this variation in human resources.

This approach may seem distasteful to our contemporary views but the methods are well known to us. They were effective, appropriate for the type of work being undertaken, and reflected the societal attitudes of the time. Conditions such as social hierarchy, domestic service, entitlement, and even empire were all a fact of life back then. Much of recent leadership practice has been viewed as holding on to that industrial manufacturing past, in keeping with Frederick Winslow Taylor's views of leadership that were established in the Age of Steel.[1] Arguably, these practices are not even leadership but straightforward management activity.

Often the terms leadership and management, or leader and manager, are used interchangeably, but there has been a long-running debate about how they differ.[2] Organisations using a traditional style of management typically see workers as order takers with limited problem-solving abilities, focused on delivering tasks to deadlines. Tasks are typically manual roles controlled through a set of processes, measured against targets, and managers inspect their work.

This does not involve any leadership, however, as there is no focus on the 'why', or organisational purpose. Essentially, management is associated with order and stability whereas leadership is associated with adaptive and constructive change.[3] In adaptive organisations, leaders are now required to be problem solvers, in the work with the feature teams and labs and acting on the knowledge to deliver meaningful products to the customers in an efficient way.

Let's revisit an area we covered in a previous chapter, when we looked at how the Cynefin Framework could be used to highlight different domains. The framework looks at four domains:

1. Complicated

2. Complex
3. Chaotic
4. Obvious or Simple

Each of the domains requires a different approach to solve problems. For some time, there has been a recognition that the objectives and activities in software development align to the characteristics of the complicated domain. But the challenge of removing the causes of waste to improve the flow of value also fits with the characteristics of the complex domain. The demands of uncertainty, ambiguity, and the need for adaptation demands new leadership. During a transformation and the pursuit of reducing waste, the majority of resistance will come from the current management, who strive for order, stability and certainty.

The solution to this problem has its roots in the evolution of military theory in the nineteenth century. Around the time that manufacturing was introducing standardisation and uniformity, military theory was moving away from a mechanistic view of units and formations. The battlefield, it was realised, was not ordered like a game of chess. And so a new theory was created by a Prussian general, Carl von Clausewitz, drawing on his experience in the Napoleonic Wars (including being on the losing side in the Battle of Jena-Auerstedt!).[4] A key part of this was the concept of 'the fog of war', i.e. that battle involves dealing with incomplete, dubious and often erroneous information.

Stephen Bungay, author of *The Art of Action: How Leaders Close the Gaps between Plans, Actions and Results*, gives an excellent description of how Carl von Clausewitz's theory was taken up and applied by the Prussians, particularly von Moltke, another survivor of the Napoleonic Wars. It demanded a new style of military leadership, which enabled decision-making and encouraged the use of initiative. Counter-intuitively for the military, it no longer accepted blind obedience to orders but instead encouraged consistency in the logic applied to problems faced on the battlefield.

This military style of leadership survives today in the workplace in the form of common guidance. Some of the guidance offered to leaders who must navigate complex environments includes:[5]

- Repeating what you did last time will not give the same outcomes—context recognition is problematic.
- Obtaining different perspectives on a problem and involving more people in the decision-making is advantageous but must be balanced with the challenges of larger groups and circumstances where time is not readily available.
- Expect to be wrong (or at least not completely right); decisions can only be based on our best current understanding, and that will always be finite and incomplete.
- The complex organisation evolves in unforeseeable ways, so the model in use may become ineffective and a 'change of mind' is advantageous, not a weakness or a sin.

Traditional organisations have been shaped by years, if not centuries, of history in the way that they are structured, operated and managed. The logic that was used when decisions were made over the years was effective, as the companies have survived. However, amongst the leadership in many of these organisations, from CEOs down to project managers, there is a growing recognition that they now operate under complex conditions, and these demand different approaches and thinking.

This need for a shift was identified in the mid-twentieth century by W. Edwards Deming.[6] In the manufacturing setting, he identified that the need to improve quality required a paradigm shift.[7] The mechanisms of control and decision-making needed to move from being the sole responsibility of those at the top to the people who did the work. The consequence of this was a de-centralisation of decision-making and more effective sensing of problems with quicker feedback loops. It resulted in many of the concepts and techniques seen in the lean movement. However, the fundamental step was that paradigm shift and a change of management logic that enabled the new techniques to be applied.

Big, long-established organisations that need to become more adaptive face the same challenge of paradigm shift. However, what is often seen in traditional organisations is a traditional response! This often involves new job titles and organisational structures, training being pushed on to employees, and culture workstreams to counter any resistance. Individuals are expected to change how they make decisions and act. Yet the management logic of top-down control is sustained through structures such as finance management, risk management, governance, KPIs and performance regimes. These can't be changed by job titles and training; they require senior leadership action. The paradigm shift is not just a challenge for those designing, building, testing and deploying the products and services, it's a challenge for all levels of leadership and management.

The leaders in organisations moving from traditional to adaptive leadership and Agile ways of working can be difficult to persuade. They are the equivalent of England cricketer Geoff Boycott, whose old-fashioned approach was perceived to be holding back the team. Getting them onside involves moving them from a fixed mindset to a growth mindset, as illustrated in Figure 9.1.

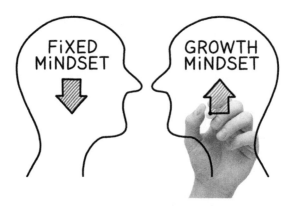

Figure 9.1 Fixed versus growth mindset

As an example of this, we worked with a Product Owner called Nia who had a fixed mindset of how to manage and deliver change for her customers. Her mindset was based on her many years of previous experience. We used open language and explained how organisations had moved on and it was Nia's choice if she wanted to change too. Over 3-6 months, we discussed how a leader's mindset sends a very powerful message to their followers that it's safe to change. Nia did this in an exceptional way by demonstrating and discussing her own vulnerabilities along the way.

Before engaging any leaders, ask yourself:

- How many 'Geoff Boycotts' do you have in your organisation?
- How would they feel about changing their leadership style?

So what are the differences between the traditional 'Geoff Boycott'-style leaders and adaptive 'Ian Bothams'? In traditional financial services companies, such as high street banks and building societies, many leaders have built their careers by applying traditional management logic over years or even decades. Moving so many individuals from traditional management logic to digital transformation, which demands new values and behaviours, is a challenge.

A key mechanism you can use is to establish an organisation-wide focus on identifying, and taking action on, the causes of waste. This enables leaders to engage in tangible action and learning, rather than being preoccupied with the utilisation of resources and the traditional view of productivity.

Of course, it's unlikely that organisations will hire whole new teams of 'Ian Bothams'. However, they will need to identify who is able to shift to the new style of leadership. Traditional logic holds that it's okay to:

- Prioritise the need to keep resources busy.
- Focus on budgets and targets rather than the work and what matters to customers.

- Ignore the things that cause work items to be blocked, as long as work is happening on something.
- Ignore work that has started but then been neglected or even abandoned before completion.

The challenge is to identify managers who are able to see the issues with the current management views and logic and focus instead on flow and value. This will result in improved effectiveness, efficiency, productivity and profit. Leaders who initiate and lead the transformation must influence and educate managers to recognise the logic and why a move away from prevailing beliefs and views is required. The need to identify the blockers, understand their causes, and establish how the feature team, lab or tribe should change, is an excellent vehicle for leadership development. There will, of course, be those that are unwilling or unable to come with you. Organisations committed to true transformation may have to make some tough decisions and look to replace their 'Geoff Boycotts' with 'Ian Bothams'.

This may be challenging for you personally. You may have leaders who are very good at delivering with traditional methods, just as Geoff Boycott was one of the most highly skilled batsmen in the world. However, as CTO, you are in place to transform the organisation with adaptive leadership. You will need to explain the difference between leaders with a traditional management style versus adaptive leadership from a number of perspectives. Some of these are summarised Table 9.1:[8]

Perspective	Traditional management	Adaptive leadership
Decision-making	Making decisions based on experience.	Making decisions based on knowledge from being in the work.

Measurement	Measurement and reporting based on financial decisions for meeting pre-agreed budget targets. Focused on keeping employees busy from a top-down project or programme plan.	Based on the flow of work and operating in an optimum way for employee motivation and speed of meaningful product to the customer. Plus, maximising the capacity of resources to keep work busy.
Motivation	Extrinsic: motivated by targets and money.	Intrinsic: self-motivated to do the right thing for the customers.
Ethos	A focus on management of people and budgets.	Acting on the system of change based on knowledge of the system.
Organisational focus	Driven by a contractual focus towards customers.	Driven to action by what matters to customers.
Organisational structure	Vertical: Hierarchical with a top-down layered structure.	Horizontal: allowing it to look at itself from the outside in.
Role of leaders	Manage the people and budgets and measure them against targets, activities and standards. Separated from the work.	Manage the work, being as close to it as possible, acting on knowledge of the system.

Role of workers	Order takers and acting on what is being received in the form of a 'tell' from leadership. Not allowed to think.	Empowered to make decisions; acting on knowledge of delivering on customer needs.

Table 9.1 Perspectives shown in Traditional versus Adaptive Leaders

One tell-tale sign of a traditional management approach is when you see individuals in the work being told what to do by leaders outside of the work. The leadership measures are based on targets, budgets and resource utilisation, not around the product being built for the customer.

This may not seem controversial, but you cannot underestimate the inertia that develops for leaders. After all, they have spent years focusing on budgets, delivery dates and targets, and making decisions with no proximity to the actual work or issues affecting the work. However, organisational transformations are not solely dependent on the executive vision and intent. In order for teams and work to be undertaken in a new way, intent must be executed effectively through the management layers. This requires managers to go on their own transformational journey and become adaptive leaders.

From our experience, the components essential to the successful transformation from traditional managers to adaptive leaders are that each individual manager has:

- Clarity on where the organisation is heading and why (not just digital transformation for the sake of it).
- A clear expectation that transformation requires a collective change of beliefs and behaviours amongst all managers.
- Psychological safety for managers to change and learn.
- Space (time and capacity) for managers to learn and adopt new leadership behaviours.
- Clear direction in the actions required for their individual learning.

- Somebody to assist them in their learning.
- Somebody to hold them accountable for their learning.

Above all, managers need to see for themselves the compelling need for why the organisation, and they as individuals, need to transform. As leaders, they can enable the organisation to become stronger and more sustainable.

ESTABLISHING THE NEED

Paradoxically, in order to establish the adaptive leadership needed by teams, leaders will need their teams to help them in their own learning journey. In earlier chapters, we outlined activity with teams to get insight and data about the blockers and waste impacting performance. Your next step should be to identify a leader from one of those teams, i.e. a Product Owner or Tribe leader, and arrange to have an informal discussion with them. Your goal is to minimise the fear and threat that can come from a conversation that spans the hierarchical levels. Here are some topics you might find useful to cover:

- Share the intent that you're attempting to identify waste and seeking to remove it.
- Explain that, in turn, you expect that this will release capacity in their area. However, this is not a cost optimisation, budget reduction or 'shrinkage' exercise.
- Recognise that what might be found could be shocking, but that this is no reflection on them as a leader. Rather, it's a common characteristic found in many organisations.
- To leverage and benefit from the insight, their leadership is necessary.
- Explore how they currently spend time in their role. In order to achieve the desired benefit, decisions may be required to 'give

up and replace' some of their current activity with new learning and improvement activity. This may be something they will need your help with.

- Make it clear that improvement is a 'team sport'. Should they encounter causes and conditions they can't influence, emphasise that you will assist and take action.

The purpose of this discussion is not to transmit a set of orders to the leader, but to help them make an informed choice about their involvement. That way, they are able to commit fully to the transformation and not feel compelled to comply for survival's sake. If there is not a wholehearted engagement, you will still have learned from the discussion. You can then pick another area and have another discussion with the next prospective leader. This may feel a lot harder, and take more effort, than just telling someone that they have a new task. However, it is much more effective to work with someone who wants to change.

Using the insight that came from the team and the study from earlier chapters, look at the following findings together:

1. Waste types identified
   - Number of days lost by type.
   - Number of work (Jira) tickets blocked.
2. Categories of causes
   - Number of days lost by category.
   - Number of work (Jira) tickets blocked.

The conversation should help the leader recognise that the objective is to identify how to resolve the blockages and the causes of blockage. This is different from the organisation's current response, which is to flag and escalate through issue- and risk-management mechanisms. The language and behaviours used by leaders in conversation are important enablers when it comes to acting on the knowledge gained.

And yet no matter how much you try to create a psychologically safe environment, leaders may still have worries and concerns. This is understandable, so go ahead and ask what the leader is feeling. The discussion will take place at the outset of the leader's own personal transformation and it is worth recognising the theory around the impact of change. Where possible, encourage their movement from shock to experimentation as quickly as possible. The move to experimentation not only develops capability but clearly involves action, which is the only way that improvement can happen.

Working through data, experimenting and taking action may not be an easy thing for leaders to do. Partnering them with a coach or change agent can be very helpful to facilitate learning and to ensure the principles of flow are applied in practice. The initial successes in addressing blockers and removing waste provide an important case study and pattern for the organisation. It also provides a compelling story of what can be achieved if the pattern is repeated and what is possible in the organisation's future.

WHO NEEDS TO KNOW?

In previous chapters, we covered the far-reaching impact that blockers can have and how various interests in different areas are affected. When it comes to storytelling, be sure to include elements that are of interest to these different areas in your case study. Table 9.2 provides some examples.

Area	Roles	Why
Business sponsors	Make decisions on funding and investment in ideas and opportunities to improve outcomes for your organisation and its customers. They have responsibility for improving profitability and reputation.	It's going to be a real shock to them to discover that, potentially, 50% of funding has been lost to waste. Not to mention the extent to which desired outcomes have been delayed and the impact waste has on predictable delivery.
Product Owners	Responsible for prioritising what is worked on so that delivery of value is achieved through product development. They may also be accountable for how investment is spent.	The waste caused by blockers slows the development of products and therefore also affects the feedback time from customers. Feedback is critical to learning what the customer likes and dislikes about your products. The blockers and waste also increase the variation in how long work takes to complete. Predicting when solutions, features and products will be completed becomes much more difficult. Where the PO is accountable for the investment, capacity wasted on work that never completes becomes a concern.

Supplier management / Legal / Procurement	Negotiate, agree and manage contracts and relationships with third parties, partners and suppliers.	Just as it's shocking to find that investment in capacity is wasted, it's equally shocking to discover similar waste spending on third parties. Or worse, the way in which the engagement and relationship is running causes blockages and waste.
		These roles should take an interest in why these problems occurred despite putting a lot of effort into the contract and working agreements. What allowed it to happen and why wasn't it spotted in the relationship management? Could something different have been designed into the formal arrangements?
		The organisation may always be dependent on suppliers, so there needs to be collective learning about how to get the best from them so that the organisation is not constrained in its speed to market.

| Board members | Develop and execute strategies that maintain the profitability, reputation and longevity of the business while building the company's value. | The extent of waste caused by blockers will invariably pose a risk to the successful execution of the strategy and its goals. The board will use a mechanism to track the progress of their strategy (potentially OKRs).[9] The blockers will slow the pace of delivery and thus the time to achieve objectives. How early can this be spotted? What are the implications for shareholders and investors? What messaging might be required? |
| Value Streams, Customer journeys, labs, feature teams and tribes | To complete work that delivers the right outcomes for customers, roles in these areas deliver what matters to the customers and create value for them. | The individuals in these teams experience frustration and disruption when trying to fulfil their roles and complete their work. They now know that there's a way of removing the cause of their frustration. These individuals have the closest proximity to the work and are therefore the first to sense the blockers. This provides an extensive sensing network that is a key source of data on blockers, waste and delay. Without their engagement, you will be operating blind in your efforts to transform the organisation. |

Table 9.2 Why waste is important to people in different roles and the impact

EXERCISE: EMPATHY MAPPING

Having spent time with one feature team or tribe, you've discovered that between 500 and 1,000 days are wasted every year due to work items being blocked. You uncovered this understanding using the knowledge-gathering techniques we covered in earlier chapters. Now, you can show that 50% of your organisation's capacity is being sapped by waste.

If your change budget is 250 million then 125 million is wasted each year and therefore not delivering the desired value to clients. If you are shocked by this, just think how stakeholders will react! Given that a variety of roles will be affected, your storytelling about the situation should be adjusted accordingly.

Some of the roles involved in an organisation's transformational journey are:

- Board members
- Business sponsors
- Product Owners
- Supplier management
- Legal
- Team members
- Scrum Masters

To consider problems from the perspective of these different people, we recommend a storytelling tool called empathy mapping. By considering their likely responses, you can develop a holistic view of the message that needs to be communicated. Your messaging should highlight problems and opportunities, which are labelled as pains and gains in Figure 9.2. For each stakeholder (persona) listed below, complete an empathy map by working through each perspective in the diagram.

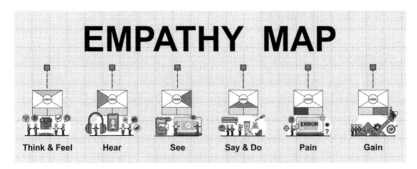

Figure 9.2 Creating an empathy map process view

REDUCING FEAR

For each stakeholder (persona), you should now have an empathy map as shown in Figure 9.3. The role/persona is in the middle of the map. It is very useful tool because in everything you do, you should look to build and maintain trust, establish psychological safety and reduce fear.

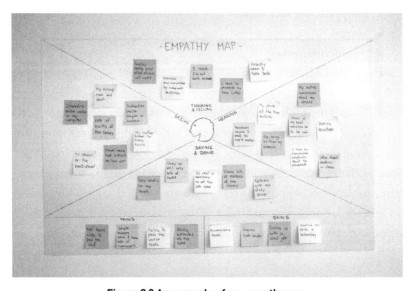

Figure 9.3 An example of an empathy map

Your organisation has many other roles and stakeholders, each with different responsibilities, needs and perspectives, that are beyond your direct remit. Your role is to help them understand the challenges and opportunities that come with the transformation. Remember that colleagues may be used to a traditional approach so leading them on the journey will be key. In the next chapter, we'll explore effective problem-solving.

TAKEAWAYS

⇨ The organisation's purpose needs to be clear and understood by its leadership.

⇨ Recognise that your existing leadership needs to change their behaviours to become adaptive. Not all existing leaders will be able to adapt.

⇨ Your leaders need an open mindset to embrace change to remove waste and increase capacity. They have the opportunity to grow individually as well as increase the organisation's capacity to deliver.

⇨ Behaviour flows from the leadership, thus it's important to them to understand how their lab, team or tribe operates and know what is slowing it down.

⇨ Behaviours of the leadership are as important, if not more so, than the actions taken to maintain and build psychological safety for all.

⇨ Choose your leadership and don't be afraid to change its behaviours, via training or replacement.

⇨ Leaders need to be aware of the impacts they have on the other elements of the organisation.

⇨ Make the organisation aware that removing waste is a team sport that includes its leaders collectively.

CHAPTER 10

THE ART OF PROBLEM SOLVING

MAKING THE INVISIBLE TANGIBLE THROUGH DATA is a vital first step in making waste visible. After that comes analysis to make sense of the data and identify where problems originate and the impact they are having. However, these alone will not lead to improvement. Without action being taken to change the way the work is currently completed, the time to get product to market will still be longer than necessary.

The next step is therefore deciding what action to take, what should be changed, how to make the changes, and confirming that the actions and changes have had the intended effect. This is the art of problem-solving. Problem-solving has been an inherent part of our nature and evolution for centuries, from early humans' use of tools to medical advances improving our life expectancy.

In this book, we've provided techniques for finding and reducing waste to improve flow and organisational performance. While that's not easy, the problem-solving stage is far trickier. In our experience, understanding and learning how to take effective action is one of the most challenging parts of the improvement journey.

This chapter will explore what the art of problem-solving entails, as well as why it is so difficult and what makes it so challenging. It will also introduce frameworks and structures to help you learn and develop the capability of problem-solving.

Despite problem-solving being an inherent part of human nature, our modern context throws up a number of significant challenges. In his Katacon Europe 2021 presentation, Nigel Thurlow explains the behavioural cause. From an early age, it is normal to be taught to win and not to lose.[1] This is reinforced through formal and informal education, such as competing with peers to obtain the highest exam grades. Plus, there's the celebration of power and success in business and sport. These things aren't bad in themselves but winning-focused behaviour has a negative impact on organisational performance and improvement.

This is something that Chris Argyris, a business theorist at Harvard Business School, also recognised and described as part of his Model 1 characteristics.[2] Argyris described two models that characterise what inhibits or enables effective organisational learning and improvement ('double-loop learning'). Model 1 outlines what inhibits learning and improvement and Argyris describes its governing variables as:

- Win, do not lose.
- Suppress negative feelings.
- Emphasise rationality.
- Achieve the purpose as the actor defines it.

This model is accompanied by another common norm. That is, success is seen as rising through the hierarchy and achieving trappings such as higher pay, benefits and status. These modes of operating have not always been detrimental to organisational performance and success. In the more ordered domains of nineteenth and twentieth century manufacturing, these behaviours did not inhibit, and may even have contributed to, success.[3]

Over many years, 'muscle memory', or repeating patterns of behaviour, have built up in organisations over time, including:

- Funding is potentially on an annual cycle.
- Funding is allocated but not aligned to the flow of work or value.
- The organisation has no idea of the costs of what is preventing it from delivering but all the reporting metrics to the board are green, so everyone is happy.

However, the nature of knowledge work is far more likely to require operating in the complex domain. Or else organisations and processes that should be in ordered domains are having to function in the complex domain, due to our designs and approaches. In these cases, the Model 1 behaviour will inhibit improvement and potentially survival. Again, Nigel Thurlow (along with Brian Rivera and John Turner) provides an excellent antidote to these modern-day challenges.[4] He places a clear emphasis on collaboration to enable success which is achieved, in part, through respect for others and distributed leadership.

Another type of challenge to effective problem-solving in organisations is the fact that we face different types of problems, which demand different approaches to deal with. A good way of approaching this is the Cynefin Framework mentioned in previous chapters.[5]

Given the challenges outlined, it is no wonder that there are a number of things that can go wrong when problem-solving, such as:

- Not understanding the type of problem and therefore using the wrong approach to tackle it (you wouldn't want a surgeon operating on you using an iterative approach!).
- We make decisions without data.
- We take only one perspective on the problem.
- Focusing on the effect, or point of contact, of a problem and not the root cause.
- Assuming that there is only one root cause of a problem.

- Trying to identify root causes when faced with a complex problem.
- Assuming a chosen solution will work.
- Being unaware of the consequences of our solutions.
- Not learning and adjusting our approaches to problem-solving.

When we looked at flagging waste data in an earlier chapter, we referred to Taylor's approach to improvement as outlined in his work. Although problematic in its application in modern times, it was grounded in a more universally applicable tenet: the scientific method.[6] Scientific method also featured as a key principle in the industrial management training and education led by the Americans in post-war Japan. It enabled a new approach to problem-solving in its efforts to improve quality and reliability.

The scientific method continues to be applied as a core principle to problem-solving and is often positioned as the basis for methods such as Plan/Do/Check/Act or the empiricism proposed in Scrum. But while science is a common feature of most people's education, it's curious that most of us never learn what the scientific method actually means when we're at school. So for clarity, what we are referring to is described in Wikipedia:[7]

At the heart of scientific method is reasoning, of which three types are defined: deductive, inductive and abductive. Understanding these different types is very helpful when recognising the different types of problems faced, the circumstances in which they occur, and the different approaches needed to address them.

Deductive - This starts with facts or known data; effective analysis of the data will then generate the solution. In iterative product development, each iteration generates feedback. This provides the data needed to identify the next iteration of the product.

Inductive - This begins with observations, which are used to form a hypothesis. By running experiments, the activity generates data and enables the experiment to be evaluated. This is the basis of empiricism. It is an intended feature of product design, whereby customer behaviour and experience are observed and used to hypothesise what will improve experiences and outcomes for customers.

Abductive - Where an idea is formed on a hunch or intuition, there is no data available or the opportunity to make observations. Abductive reasoning tests the mental model and assumptions associated with the idea. The generation of concepts and products such as MP3 players or Facebook are examples of this reasoning.

Common techniques for 'solving' business problems, including A3, 8D and DMAIC, are described in terms of steps and processes.[8] Yet it can be hard to see how the steps should be applied in different ways according to different problems, and therefore which type of reasoning is being applied. Experienced problem-solvers have learnt that the application is not as linear as the steps and process suggest.

This appears to be a common issue when individuals and teams use the A3 approach developed in Toyota.[9] When teams are trained to use A3, completing it can become the focus in itself. The intended purpose of A3 is to share the logic, reasoning and decisions applied to a problem, as well as the learning obtained in tackling it. When individuals and teams are seeking to use the scientific method for improvement, and therefore the art of problem-solving, a coaching approach to developing that ability is more effective than straightforward training.

One of the other challenges is that some of the factors and causes relating to the problem may be intangible. Again, Argyris' work on organisational performance and the importance of double-loop learning are helpful to highlight and address flawed assumptions, beliefs and logic. It's not good for leaders to believe that keeping resources busy is in the interests of productivity as this can lead to sub-optimisation of flow. It's more important to keep work busy.

As an example, in one area we found teams were having to batch together work that required a suite of non-functional testing. The logic was that conducting the testing for all the teams on a monthly basis was 'cheaper' than allowing each team to undertake testing fortnightly or even weekly. But the policy created a constraint in the flow of work. It resulted in work queuing and being delayed, increasing the lead time. Ironically the 'cost' was only the cross-charging between internal teams and therefore had no true impact on the organisation's profit and loss account.

APPROACH

Having outlined the issues and challenges involved in problem-solving being formulaic, there is still a need to introduce some structure to illustrate how problems can be approached. Learning how to adapt the structure and methods depending on the problem type and circumstances comes with practice and experience.

Scientific method provides the basis of the structure and involves observation, data, creating hypotheses and running experiments to learn about the hypotheses. Action is taken based on the learning, and further iterations of hypothesis and experiments may be required to get to the desired goal. Elements that are likely to prove helpful when addressing problems are:

- Summarising the current situation, providing background and context to build a common situational awareness amongst those involved in addressing the problem.
- Describing the ultimate goal in relation to the problem and therefore what the ideal situation is. The gap between the

current and the ideal clarifies the problem and data can then be gathered to quantify it.

- Breaking the problem down and finding the root cause.
- Analysing the problem to identify root causes.
- Identifying containment (actions to minimise the impact) and counter-measures (actions to remove the problem and mitigate the risk of it reoccurring).
- Testing and evaluating counter-measures.
- Implementing a solution and monitoring for effectiveness.

As an illustration of breaking the problem down, imagine a server used for a type of testing. You find that the server is repeatedly not available and often requires a restart. On investigation, you find that it's repeatedly running out of memory. The lack of memory required to complete necessary tasks is an example of a point of cause. The actual root cause might be an error in the original infrastructure design (i.e. the server was built with insufficient storage), or it could be the design of the application and the code quality. It may be both or other causes besides!

When faced with a problem in the ordered domains, data may exist that enables deductive reasoning to be applied. When the relevant skill, knowledge and expertise is connected to the data, analysis can reveal the root causes. Appropriate solutions can then be deployed because good practice can be repeated from previous experience.

In the domains that are not ordered (complex, chaotic, disordered), previous experience and repetitions of previously successful solutions are unlikely to return the same desired outcomes. In domains where observations can be made, inductive reasoning can be applied. This enables hypotheses to be formed. Hypotheses can be tested and data collected to evaluate them and move the problem into ordered domains. In the absence of observations, inductive reasoning is required, which enables observations to be made and further reasoning applied.

The consequences of problems in different domains requiring different reasoning means that the elements of problem-solving listed above need variation in their sequence. They may not be in a linear order. Examples of the variation in approach are outlined by Karen Martin, author of *Value Stream Mapping* in one of her posts on LinkedIn.[10]

PROBLEM SCENARIO

To bring the elements to life in one particular sequence, here is an example of a problem that we encountered.

Current situation

Our team feels under pressure to take on more work. We're already busy, and things seem to be taking longer to complete. Because it is taking longer, we're being chased for completion, which is adding more pressure. The ultimate goal in relation to the problem is that we want to pull work into the team at the rate we are able to complete it. We want work items completed in a shorter time, with no ageing or neglected work-in-progress (WIP).

Currently, we take in work items at a rate of 17 in each time box, but are completing them at a rate of 12 in each time box. At the beginning of the increment (quarter 2), we had a WIP of 5 items. As we start the new increment (quarter 3), we have a WIP of 42 items. The average time to complete an item is currently 5 days, with an upper control limit of 19 days. Team happiness was recently polled and found to be 3.2, which is down from 4.1 at the beginning of the quarter.

Point of cause of the problem

The amount of work that is planned for each time box as a result of the decisions made in the planning activity.

Root causes identified

Planning is done by the team leader and validated (approved) by the business stakeholder accountable for the outcomes relating to the product. Decisions are made using the expected completion dates of the various initiatives that the team is working on. Decisions are not made by considering the team's capacity and throughput. There are no policies about the amount of WIP in the different flow states.

Containment

The team proposed that for the next timebox, no new work was taken on. They worked on clearing the existing WIP, tackling the oldest items first. This was rejected by the business stakeholder as a containment measure because it was seen as too much of a delivery risk for a priority initiative.

Counter-measures

Take the business stakeholder through an education piece about flow. Have the planning activity involve the team's Scrum Master. Planning is to be based on capacity and throughput data. The team should develop the WIP limit policy and use it to apply and manage WIP in each flow state. Team retros should use a cumulative flow diagram to reflect on the efficacy of planning decisions and WIP limits.

Test and evaluate counter-measures

By the end of the increment (quarter 3), the rate in and rate out of work is stable at 15 items in each timebox. WIP is currently 12, with no item having started earlier than the previous timebox. The average time to complete an item is currently 3 days, with an upper control limit of 9 days.[11] Team happiness was recently polled at 4.3.

MOMENTUM

Acquiring new abilities happens through learning, and developing the ability to deal with problems effectively is no different. It does not happen instantly, however. In your role as CTO, you can play an active role in recognising this and creating conditions to enable learning and improvement.

The acquisition of information, actions and experience can be slow to begin with. It may mean working slowly and methodically through the first few problems. By doing so, you'll learn how to recognise different types of problems, determine the appropriate sequence of problem-solving elements, frame hypotheses, and identify data and measurements for evaluating the outcomes of experiments. You should help teams reflect on the approach taken in addressing the problem. You can set expectations and give teams assurance about the initial need for rigorous learning rather than resolving problems quickly.

In earlier chapters, we recognised that people who complete the activities and work of product development and creation are the ones who best understand the data and its context. These individuals are best placed to address the problems causing blockages, delay and other waste. Establishing this ownership and amending roles to include responsibility for improving future delivery, rather than just enabling current delivery, is another way you can help. This will help you manage the capacity of teams, the flow load, and the WIP they can manage.

Establishing ownership also results in teams owning the key data needed to identify and tackle problems. The need for an accurate reflection and record of reality leads to consistency and discipline in the use of workflow and management tools such as Jira. This becomes more evident and intrinsic to the teams, so that the metrics they use pass the test of good measurement.

However, simply telling a team that they are empowered just won't cut it, particularly when the conditions that prevent them from being empowered remain the same. One initial approach to signalling owner-ship is to get the team to answer the following questions for themselves:

- Of the problems and waste they have learnt about, what is it that they would like to change?
- How would they like to approach the change?
- What support, resource or input do they need from you or other leaders?

How you respond as a leader to the intent and decisions made by the team is the real signalling of ownership. Efforts at this stage to get the teams to explain and justify their decisions will signal that the locus of control and real ownership of the problem still sits within the man-agement hierarchy. As long as teams are not selecting an approach that would result in physical harm, damage the reputation of the company or break any laws, effective learning will happen, regardless of whether or not the improvement is impactful.

Proof that effective change can happen is a powerful mechanism for building momentum and confidence in teams and the organisation that problems can be tackled and tangible improvements made. In order to help with this, it may be that teams start by tackling smaller and less significant problems. If teams take on the causes of blockers and waste under their control and influence, this may help them learn about prob-lem-solving, even though successful resolution may not have the biggest impact on the end-to-end flow. This can be the case where the end-to-end flow consists of multiple teams, with numerous handovers needed to get work and flow items to a 'Done' state.

If one team senses the problem but the problem is related to activity in another team, both teams will need to be involved in dealing with the problem. Leaders play an important role in bridging organisational structures and boundaries to bring together the necessary perspectives, insights, knowledge and capabilities. Creating the conditions that enable individuals from disparate teams to form a bespoke team to swarm on a problem rarely happens intuitively. For bigger problems spanning a greater number of teams, or where problems are complex, the need for diversity of perspectives is critical to success.[12] It requires effective leadership to enable the right conditions.

Building problem-solving in a team, and the teams they are connected to, provides a basis for building momentum through the organisation. As the initial teams work through problems and generate results, it creates storytelling collateral. This can help other leaders and teams understand the benefit of investing time and effort in developing storytelling capacity. Key stories frame the learning that must be shared to generate the intrinsic desire and motivation needed for effective transformation. Stories that need to be shared are:

- The problems identified and the solutions to them.
- Impact of effective problem-solving.
- How the data about flow, waste and blockers enabled the problem to be identified.
- How the problem-solving capability was developed.

In traditional organisations, corporate information flow, including relevant organisational learning, follows hierarchical structures and pathways. However, this can affect the benefit gained from information sharing. Learning is slowed and subject to filtering and disruption as it passes between hierarchical layers. In some cases, it is not passed on and fails to reach those who would benefit from the insight. It is therefore important to not only create stories but identify mechanisms for sharing them. In some cases, elements of the Spotify approach are introduced to organisations so that tribes, guilds and communities could prove helpful in story sharing (Spotify had success with the implementation of Agile).[13]

One of the earliest examples of sharing learning between teams, rather than through hierarchies, was in the First World War.[14] The practice was documented in a case study by Dr Robert T. Foley of the Defence Studies Department at King's College London. Besides being an early example of adaptation in a complex domain, there are two more useful things we can take from the case study: the horizontal innovation, including the lessons learned system, and learning culture.

The German army innovated by spreading knowledge between units rather than up and down the chain of command. This changed how it fought in the midst of battle. Units engaged in fighting would, as soon as possible after leaving the frontline, create an 'experience' report. This would be shared rapidly with other units in the front line and with those preparing to join the front line.

The experience reports did not follow a set format but essentially contained 'lessons learned' that focused on what worked and what didn't. They were analytical and uncompromisingly honest, which was normal for the German army. A strong learning culture permeated the organisation, having been established years before the start of the war. Although Germany ultimately lost the war, the defeat was due to strategic ineptitude. The army is recognised as having been operationally effective.

Learning fast is a key concept in adaptive, Agile organisations. However, there are many examples where experimentation and 'learning by failing fast' have been impeded by a lack of psychological safety.[15] Important learning about what does not work is blocked by teams and individuals hiding activity and the consequences of the activity. What has surprised us is that teams can even be reluctant to show successful results, which demonstrates just how impactful organisational norms can be in disrupting open and honest dialogue.

The case study also highlights that effective sharing of learning was by written reports with no requirement to follow a standardised format. This is contrary to received wisdom about the importance of A3 standard formats. In our story-sharing, we are not limited to a written medium but can now share learning through a variety of media and formats such as webinars, podcasts and videos.

Learning and having knowledge will provide you with problems that need solving in order to improve the performance of the organisation. A key enabler in building momentum in your organisation's problem-solving and improvement efforts is naturally to measure it. Obvious measures include how many problems have been worked on, how many are currently being worked on, and the size of the backlog of known problems. The balance between work for customers and improvement efforts to remove waste and increase capacity is important.

It's useful to measure how much capacity is invested by teams. Just as the work done for customers can be disrupted, affecting flow and time to complete the work, the same is true for problem-solving. You've probably already recognised that the time it takes to resolve a problem, as well as what prevents progress, are useful measurements. Other measures that might contribute to momentum include the cumulative impact of the resolved problems on things like reducing lead time, reducing operating cost, and increasing throughput.

The measured impact could even extend to colleague satisfaction and morale, either from being engaged in problem-solving or the consequences of successful problem resolution. As with any other metric, measurement is only useful in a learning context. If the metrics are used for coercion and control, there is an increased risk of 'gaming' the data in the absence of psychological safety. Again, this is an important role for you to play to ensure an effective learning environment is created and maintained.

Just as in any endeavour that requires the application of theories and principles, achieving it is challenging and even more difficult if tackled in isolation. Whether it is through effective learning and reflective groups or via the more focused and deliberate involvement of a coach, it is extremely beneficial to have an external and supportive perspective to enable the required reflection, appraisal and learning.

As CTO, you can be critical to the success of your organisation. By providing empowerment and a desire to problem-solve, you can influence culture and behaviour. By putting the right foundations in place, you can find, theme and quantity waste. At the same time, you'll have measures to deal with resistance from Scrum Masters like Ruth and leaders with a 'Geoff Boycott' mindset.

If you and your organisation have started thinking about waste and are curious about it, you are well on your way to tracking down its causes and proudly calling yourself a Waste Detective.

You've come with us this far, so we'd like to give you a virtual high five and wish you every success in removing waste and increasing capacity.

TAKEAWAYS

⇨ Organisational muscle memory can cause problems of budgets not aligned to value, or flow of works to the customer.

⇨ Organisations have no, or limited, idea of the costs that prevent delivery.

⇨ Organisations are impacted by a variety of problems, making it difficult to get to their root causes.

⇨ Understanding the different types of reasoning (deductive, inductive and abductive) is very helpful when recognising the different types of problems faced.

⇨ Build problem-solving into the teams and collaborate across the organisation to build enthusiasm to resolve the problems.

⇨ Visibility, honesty and sharing of what is blocked in the teams is essential and forms a key part of organisational behaviour.

NOTES

Chapter 1

1. Jira Software: A suite of agile work management solutions from Atlassian. Kanban: A popular framework used in software development that visually represents work items on a physical whiteboard or a software product such as Jira.
2. Jill Duffy (2016), 'How Much Time Do We Lose Task-Switching?', Productivity Report: Bridging Research And Practice On Personal Productivity. [https://productivityreport. org/2016/02/22/how-much-time-do-we-lose-task-switching/]

Chapter 2

1. Hiren Doshi (2016), 'The Three Pillars of Empiricism (Scrum)', Scrum.org. [https://www.scrum.org/resources/blog/ three-pillars-empiricism-scrum]
2. A feature team is an enduring team that produces meaningful product delivery to its customers in the form of new, usable features. There can be a few or many of these teams in an organisation. See https://less.works/less/structure/feature-teams

Chapter 3

1. Definition of retrospective, The 2020 Scrum Guide. [https://scrumguides.org/scrum-guide.html#sprint-retrospective]
2. Daniel Vacanti (2015), *Actionable Agile Metrics For Predictability: An Introduction*
3. Niklas Modig and Par Ahlstrom (2012), *This is Lean: Resolving the Efficiency Paradox*—see the chapter on resource versus flow efficiency.
4. Getkanban, a board game for training Scrum Masters.
5. J. R. P. French, Jr., and B. Raven (1959), 'The bases of social power', Studies in social power
6. Mary Poppendieck (2006), Implementing Lean Software Development: From Concept to Cash
7. Niklas Modig and Par Ahlstrom (2012), *This is Lean: Resolving the Efficiency Paradox*—see brief description of second order.
8. The Monkey Business Illusion (2010), Daniel Simons, YouTube. [https://youtu.be/IGQmdoK_ZfY]
9. John Seddon (2019), *Beyond Command and Control*
10. Russell L. Ackoff, Herbert J. Addison and Sally Bibb (2007), *Management f-Laws: How Organizations Really Work*
11. Mark K. Smith (2001, 2013), 'Chris Argyris: theories of action, double-loop learning and organizational learning.' [https://infed.org/mobi/chris-argyris-theories-of-action-double-loop-learning-and-organizational-learning/]
12. John Seddon (2003), *Freedom from Command and Control: A Better Way to Make the Work Work*
13. Our experience seems to align with Kotter's 8-step change model, although we didn't deliberately design our approach using the model.
14. Chin and Benne - seminal paper published in 1969 by Chin and Benne, 'General Strategies for Effecting Changes in Human Systems'.

15. Chris Argyris (1970), *Intervention Theory and Method: A Behavioral Science View*
16. Leon Festinger (1957), *A Theory of Cognitive Dissonance*
17. Kubler-Ross Change Curve in Paul Turner (2021), *The Making of the Modern Manager: Mapping Management Competencies from the First to the Fourth Industrial Revolution*
18. Chin and Benne - seminal paper published in 1969 by Chin and Benne, 'General Strategies for Effecting Changes in Human Systems'.

Chapter 4

1. Bounded Applicability and Cynefin, Cynefin.io. [https://cynefin.io/wiki/Cynefin]
2. Business Agility, Scaled Agile, Inc. [https://www.scaledagile-framework.com/business-agility/]
3. Frederick Winslow Taylor and scientific management, Wikipedia. [https://en.wikipedia.org/wiki/Scientific_management]
4. Alfred P. Sloan's functional structuring of GM in Divisions and cost centres discussed in 'The Great GM Mystery', Harvard Business Review. [https://hbr.org/1964/09/the-great-gm-mystery]
5. Complex Doman and the Cynefin Framework, Cynefin.io. [https://thecynefin.co/]
6. Varun Tripathi et al (2021). 'An Agile System to Enhance Productivity through a Modified Value Stream Mapping Approach in Industry 4.0: A Novel Approach', Sustainability. [https://www.mdpi.com/2071-1050/13/21/11997]

Chapter 5

1. Frederick Winslow Taylor (1911), *The Principles of Scientific Management*

2. General Stanley McChrystal, David Silverman, et al. (2015), *Team of Teams: New Rules of Engagement for a Complex World*
3. Chapter 3, page 61 in John Seddon (2003), *Freedom from Command and Control: A Better Way to Make the Work Work*
4. Andy Brogan (2018), 'A Little Blog about Purpose', Easier Inc. [https://www.easierinc.com/blog/a-little-blog-about-purpose/#:~:text=It%20connects%20people%20with%20the,compass%20point%20for%20their%20ambitions]

Chapter 6

1. John Seddon (2003), *Freedom from Command and Control: A Better Way to Make the Work Work*
2. Dominica Degrandis (2017), *Making Work Visible: Exposing Time Theft to Optimize Workflow*
3. 'Cost of Delay: the Economic Impact of a Delay in Project Delivery', Kanbanize. [https://kanbanize.com/lean-management/value-waste/cost-of-delay]
4. Chapter 3, Page 77 in Mik Kirsten (2019), *Project to Product: How Value Stream Networks Will Transform IT and Business: How to Survive and Thrive in the Age of Digital Disruption with the Flow Framework*
5. 'Gil Broza - Being Agile: Having the Mindset that Delivers - 2016 The Path to Agility Conference', COHAA, YouTube. [https://www.youtube.com/watch?v=p1jT-4mkGkA]
6. Value Stream Management, Wikipedia. [https://en.wikipedia.org/wiki/Value_stream]
7. What Is Value Stream Mapping? Benefits and Implementation, Kanbanize. [https://kanbanize.com/lean-management/value-waste/value-stream-mapping]
8. Definition of efficiency, Cambridge Dictionary. [https://dictionary.cambridge.org/dictionary/english/efficiency]

9. See Chapter 4, 'The Efficiency Paradox', in Niklas Modig and Par Ahlstrom (2012), *This is Lean: Resolving the Efficiency Paradox*

10. Cost of delay, Wikipedia. [https://en.wikipedia.org/wiki/Cost_of_delay#:~:text=Cost%20of%20Delay%20is%20%22a,value%20leaks%20away%20over%20time]

11. Atlassian. [https://www.atlassian.com]

Chapter 7

1. Gil Broza (2015), *The Agile Mind-Set: Making Agile Processes Work*

2. W. Edwards Deming (1982), *Out of the Crisis*; John Seddon (2003), *Freedom from Command and Control: A Better Way to Make the Work Work*

3. Empiricism, Wikipedia. [https://en.wikipedia.org/wiki/Empiricism]

4. Cluster analysis, Wikipedia. [https://en.wikipedia.org/wiki/Cluster_analysis]

Chapter 8

1. Mik Kersten (2019), *Project to Product: How to Survive and Thrive in the Age of Digital Disruption with the Flow Framework*

2. Dr Carol Dweck (2017), *Mindset: Changing The Way You think To Fulfil Your Potential*

3. Amy C. Edmondson (2018), *The Fearless Organization: Creating Psychological Safety in the Workplace for Learning, Innovation, and Growth*

4. Dave Snowden, Riva Greenberg, et al. (2020), Cynefin - Weaving Sense-Making into the Fabric of Our *World*

Chapter 9

1. Mik Kersten (2019), *Project to Product: How to Survive and Thrive in the Age of Digital Disruption with the Flow Framework*
2. Shamas-ur-Rehman Toor and George Ofori (2008), 'Leadership versus Management: How They Are Different, and Why', Leadership and Management in Engineering, Volume 8 Issue 2. [https://ascelibrary.org/doi/full/10.1061/%28ASCE%291532-6748%282008%298%3A2%2861%29]
3. Peter G. Northouse (2018), *Leadership: Theory and Practice*
4. Carl von Clausewitz (1832), *On War*
5. Kurt A. Richardson (2008), 'Managing Complex Organizations: Complexity Thinking and the Science and Art of Management', E:CO Issue Vol. 10 No. 2 2008 p. 13-26
6. W. Edwards Deming (1982), *Out of the Crisis*
7. According to the Oxford English Dictionary, paradigm shift is "a fundamental change in approach or underlying assumptions".
8. Adapted from John Seddon's original articulation in *Freedom from Command and Control: A Better Way to Make the Work Work* (2003).
9. John Doerr (2021), *Speed & Scale: A Global Action Plan for Solving Our Climate Crisis Now*

Chapter 10

1. Katacon 2021 Presentation with Nigel Thurlow. Toyota Kata and The Flow System. https://www.youtube.com/watch?v=XZqzSEuCQ5E
2. Mark K. Smith, *Chris Argyris: theories of action, double-loop learning and organizational learning.* https://infed.org/mobi/chris-argyris-theories-of-action-double-loop-learning-and-organizational-learning/

3. Ibid.
4. Nigel Thurlow, Brian Rivera and John Turner (2021), *The Flow System: The Evolution of Agile and Lean Thinking in an Age of Complexity*
5. Cynefin is regularly updated.
6. Scientific management, Wikipedia. [https://en.wikipedia.org/wiki/Scientific_management]
7. Scientific method, Wikipedia. [https://en.wikipedia.org/wiki/Scientific_method]
8. DMAIC, Wikipedia. [https://en.wikipedia.org/wiki/DMAIC] A3 problem solving, Wikipedia. [https://en.wikipedia.org/wiki/A3_problem_solving#:~:text=A3%20problem%20solving%20is%20a,guides%20problem%20solving%20by%20workers]
   Eight disciplines (8D) problem solving, Wikipedia. [https://en.wikipedia.org/wiki/Eight_disciplines_problem_solving]
9. Toyota A3 Problem Solving Technique
10. Karen Martin, LinkedIn, https://www.linkedin.com/posts/karenmartinopex_problemsolving-rootcauseanalysis-hypothesistesting-activity-6877969764971536384-SMst
11. This is a limit that is calculated using the Statistical Process Control Chart. The limit indicates that unless there is a change in the process or system the data comes from then with 99.75% certainty the next data point will fall within the limits.
12. John R. Turner and Nigel Thurlow (2020), *The Flow System: Key Principles and Attributes*
13. Alvar Lundberg (2020), *Successful with the Agile Spotify Framework: Squads, Tribes and Chapters - The Next Step After Scrum and Kanban?*
14. Robert T. Foley (2012), 'A Case Study in Horizontal Military Innovation: The German Army, 1916–1918', Journal of Strategic Studies

15. Amy C. Edmondson (2018), *The Fearless Organization: Creating Psychological Safety in the Workplace for Learning, Innovation, and Growth*

FURTHER RESOURCES

Chapter 1

Jeff Sutherland and J.J. Sutherland (2014), *Scrum: The Art of Doing Twice the Work in Half the Time*

Caitlin Sadowski and Thomas Zimmermann (2019), *Rethinking Productivity in Software Engineering*

Chapter 2

Jeff Sutherland and J.J. Sutherland (2014), *Scrum: The Art of Doing Twice the Work in Half the Time*

Mary Walton (1986), *The Deming Management Method*

W. Edwards Deming (1982), *Out of the Crisis*

John Seddon (2014), The Whitehall Effect: How Whitehall Became the Enemy of Great Public Services - and What We Can Do About it

John Seddon (2019), *Beyond Command and Control*

Robert G. Meyers (2006), *Understanding Empiricism (Understanding Movements in Modern Thought)*

Chapter 3

Mark K. Smith (2001, 2013). 'Chris Argyris: theories of action, double-loop learning and organizational learning', *The encyclopedia of pedagogy and informal education*. [https://infed.org/mobi/chris-argyris-theories-of-action-double-loop-learning-and-organizational-learning/]

Chris Argyris, 'Intervention Theory and Methods'. [http://web.mit.edu/curhan/www/docs/Articles/15341_Readings/Organizational_Learning_and_Change/Argyris_Intervention_Theory_&_Methods_Classic_Readings_pp587-591.pdf.]

Chapter 5

Create a Pareto chart, Microsoft Support. [https://support.microsoft.com/en-us/office/create-a-pareto-chart-a1512496-6dba-4743-9ab1-df5012972856]

Dominica Degrandis (2017), *Making Work Visible: Exposing Time Theft to Optimize Workflow*

Chapter 6

Costa Stathis (2016, 2019). 'Failure Demand—Reducing Cost and Improving the Customer Experience', Call Centre Helper. [https://www.callcentrehelper.com/failure-demand-a-technique-to-reduce-cost-and-improve-the-customer-experience-91527.htm]

'Cost of Delay: the Economic Impact of a Delay in Project Delivery', Kanbanize. [https://kanbanize.com/lean-management/value-waste/cost-of-delay]'What Is Value Stream Mapping? Benefits and Implementation', Kanbanize, https://kanbanize.com/lean-management/value-waste/value-stream-mapping]

Chapter 7

'Managing Blockers & Dependencies with Data - Troy Magennis' (2020), Agile & Kanban Coaching Exchange, YouTube. [https://www.youtube.com/watch?v=f0WH75d4Oyg&t=6s]

'Gil Broza - Being Agile: Having the Mindset that Delivers - 2016 The Path to Agility Conference' (2016), COHAA, YouTube. [https://www.youtube.com/watch?v=p1jT-4mkGkA]

Chapter 8

Tasktop Flow Framework. [https://www.tasktop.com/]

Geoff Watts (2017), *Product Mastery: From Good To Great Product Ownership*

General Stanley McChrystal, David Silverman, et al. (2015), *Team of Teams: New Rules of Engagement for a Complex World*

Carol Dweck (2017), *Mindset - Updated Edition: Changing The Way You think To Fulfil Your Potential*

Google Project Aristotle and psychological safety. [https://rework.withgoogle.com/print/guides/5721312655835136/]

Dave Snowden, Riva Greenberg, et al. (2020), *Cynefin - Weaving Sense-Making into the Fabric of Our World*

Chapter 10

'Katacon 2021 Presentation with Nigel Thurlow. Toyota Kata and The Flow System' (2021), Nigel Thurlow. [https://www.youtube.com/watch?v=XZqzSEuCQ5E]

Homer M. Sarasohn and Charles A. Protzman (1998), 'The Fundamentals of Industrial Management' CCS Management Course

The Cynefin Co. [https://thecynefin.co/]

'Organizational Learning - Single and Double-Loop Learning' (2016), Brittany Tomasini. [https://www.youtube.com/watch?v=boUoxw6sphs.]

'Double-loop learning: a case study from the front-line | Roderic Yapp | TEDxWandsworth' (2016), TEDx Talks. [https://www.youtube.com/watch?v=JN6elXXSrRM]

Can we ask a small favour?

It would mean a lot to us if you could spare a moment to review this book by clicking the link below. You only need to write a couple of sentences so it won't take long.

We'd be very grateful. By leaving us a review, you'll help more people discover this book and learn about waste in their organisations. And as you can tell, we're passionate about waste and its causes and we really want to tell as many people as possible about it.

Thank you!
Brian and Richard

INDEX

ABOUT THE AUTHORS

BRIAN HOOKER

BRIAN HOOKER STUDIED CIVIL ENGINEERING PRIOR to calculating the life expectancy of motorways as a Highways Engineer in the UK and Malaysia. After realising that life on the roads wasn't for him, he studied Computer Science at the University of the West of England while working as a software developer. This started him working in transformation across a spectrum of roles, from testing, system engineering and analysis to transformational coaching. He's worked in software companies that are purely focused on their product as well as those with bespoke, enterprise-wide solutions. Brian currently works as a Business Agility Lead. Away from work, you're likely to find Brian in a wetsuit, bodyboarding at his nearest beach with his daughter. He is also a long-suffering fan of Plymouth Argyle F.C., who his late father referred to as the Manchester United of the southwest.

RICHARD MOIR

RICHARD STUDIED ELECTRONIC AND ELECTRICAL ENGINEERING at Sheffield University before starting out as a commissioned officer for 10 years in the British Army before transitioning into business change for the next 20 years. Richard then went into programme management for a number of years before moving into consultancy. He joined Vanguard Consulting, where he worked with John Seddon, author of *Beyond Command and Control*. Today, he consults on Agile and Systems Thinking as a Head Transformational Coach. Richard is a family man and keen surfer and if the conditions are right, he surfs with his sons.

Printed in Great Britain
by Amazon